Strategies of Difference
in Modern Poetry

Strategies of Difference in Modern Poetry

Case Studies in Poetic Composition

Edited by
Pierre Lagayette

Madison • Teaneck
Fairleigh Dickinson University Press
London: Associated University Presses

© 1998 by Associated University Presses, Inc.

All rights reserved. Authorization to photocopy items for internal or personal use, or the internal or personal use of specific clients, is granted by the copyright owner, provided that a base fee of $10.00, plus eight cents per page, per copy is paid directly to the Copyright Clearance Center, 222 Rosewood Drive, Danvers, Massachusetts 01923. [0-8386-3698-5/98 $10.00 + 8¢ pp, pc.]

Associated University Presses
440 Forsgate Drive
Cranbury, NJ 08512

Associated University Presses
16 Barter Street
London WC1A 2AH, England

Associated University Presses
P.O. Box 338, Port Credit
Mississauga, Ontario
Canada L5G 4L8

The paper used in this publication meets the requirements of the American National Standard for Permanence of Paper for Printed Library Materials Z39.48-1984.

Library of Congress Cataloging-in-Publication Data

Strategies of difference in modern poetry : case studies in poetic composition / edited by Pierre Lagayette.
    p.   cm.
   Includes bibliographical references and index.
   ISBN 0-8386-3698-5 (alk. paper)
   1. Poetry, Modern—History and criticism. 2. Difference (Philosophy) in literature. I. Lagayette, Pierre.
PN1136.S84 1998
809.1'9384—dc21   97-39277
                                        CIP

PRINTED IN THE UNITED STATES OF AMERICA

LIBRARY
ALMA COLLEGE
ALMA, MICHIGAN

Contents

Contributors

CHARLES ALTIERI is Professor of English at the University of California, Berkeley. He has written numerous critical studies of modern poetry. Among his best-known books are: *Enlarging the Temple,* on the poetry of the 1960s; *Self and Sensibility,* on American poetry in the 1970s; and *Painterly Abstractions in Modernist American Poetry,* on contemporary experimental poetry.

MASSIMO BACIGALUPO is Professor of American Literature at the University of Genoa, Italy, an expert on Ezra Pound, and a translator of Pound's works into Italian. He received a Ph.D. from Columbia University and has taught at Yale, Osaka, and Cambridge, England. He has authored a monograph on Pound and several essays on American poets.

GENEVIÈVE COHEN-CHEMINET is currently Professor of English at the Lycée Lakanal in Sceaux, France. She has written a doctoral thesis on Charles Reznikoff and published several articles on this poet.

GUDRUN M. GRABHER is Professor of Literature at the University of Innsbruck, Austria. She holds a doctorate in American Studies and in Philosophy and has taught at Harvard and in Japan. She has published a book-length study of Emily Dickinson, and another on American lyric poetry, both of them with the University Presses of Heidelberg, Germany.

PIERRE LAGAYETTE is currently Professor of American Studies at the University of Paris 4–Sorbonne. He received a Ph.D. in Literature from the University of California, Santa Cruz. He has written a thesis on California poet Robinson Jeffers and published several books on the American West and American history. He has taught at Santa Cruz, the University of Texas, and the University of Tennessee.

7

TATO LAVIERA is a Puerto Rican poet, born in New York City. He is the author of several important books of poetry, among which *La Carreta Made a U-Turn* and *AmeRican,* made him one of the widest-read U.S. Hispanic writers. He has taught at Rutgers University and is also a member of the Center for Puerto Rican Studies in New York.

ANNE LUYAT-MOORE is Professor of American Literature at the University of Avignon, France. She has recently published *L'Aurore boréale,* a translation of Wallace Stevens's *The Auroras of Autumn* (Bruxelles: Le Cri, 1994).

TAFFY MARTIN is currently Professor of American Literature at the University of Poitiers, France. She is the author of numerous articles on American women poets of the twentieth century. She also has published a study of Marianne Moore's poetry with the University of Texas Press, *Marianne Moore, Subversive Modernist.*

AXEL NESME is Assistant Professor of English at the University of Lyons 2, France. He has written a doctoral thesis and several articles on Theodore Roethke. He has also published new French translations of Thomas Mann's *Death in Venice* and *Tristan.*

VÉRONIQUE RAULINE is Assistant Professor of English at the University of Paris 10—Nanterre. She has written a doctoral thesis on Nuyorican poetry.

ALAIN SUBERCHICOT is Professor of American Literature at the University of Clermont-Ferrand, France. He has translated modern American and British poets into French and has published articles on William Bronk, Wallace Stevens, H. D., Thoreau, Robert Lowell, and Ralph Waldo Emerson, among others. He is currently at work on a monograph on Wallace Stevens.

Strategies of Difference
in Modern Poetry

Introduction

PIERRE LAGAYETTE

IN THE PHENOMENOLOGICAL WORLD, THE EXPERIENCE OF DIFFERENCE
is a common one. Sensory perceptions work naturally according
to principles of differentiation that can be rather easily characterized. When it comes, however, to conceptually qualifying or
systematizing difference itself we have to meet a more singularly
complex challenge. Sciences like mathematics or physics are, in
most cases, able to quantify differences and incorporate them
into their systems of rules or laws. It will be recalled here that
the very notion of quantity is wholly predicated on difference,
one given quantity existing only in ratio to all other—therefore
different—quantities. Otherness offers no bafflement to the scientist, for the world he deals with is cosmological, in which
things are identified and explained by their connections with
other things. Difference is not just distinctive but also constitutive of that world and, as an experimental constant, it may paradoxically be seen as a totalizing and unifying principle.

Difference is more unsettling to the philosopher and the poet,
for three major reasons: first, the world they describe is an an-
thropological world in which things derive their properties from
the relations they establish with ourselves. These connections
are further founded on the essential difference between "me"
and "not-me." They require the postulated alterity of consciousness from the material world. The history of metaphysics reca-
pitulates centuries of attempts to reduce that difference, to
bridge that distance we now call *écart* between being and non-
being, between man and thing. This philosophical pursuit itself
implies a loss—which contemporary philosophers have tried to
minimalize—of the immanence of thought in the real world that
constitutes its object. There must be some room left for thought
to develop, some representative or enunciative distance which,
at the same time as it allows for philosophical investigation and
explanation, reinforces the duality of subject and object. Beyond
the ontological *écart*, then, it is the whole process of representa-

11

tion that amplifies the role of difference in the work of thought. Historically, post-Spinozian philosophy has accepted the impossibility of a radical immanence of thought to the reality it conceives and has been premised on dualisms, that of being and logos, and also of subject and object. No thought is possible— except in the improbable case of mystical intuition or fusion— that would so adhere to the real as to leave no space for dualisms or mediations of some kind.

Dualisms, then, are largely responsible for the positiveness of difference as a precondition for the activity of thinking. Conversely, every conception of the real and proposition thereof bears in itself some trace of the fundamental dualism between the thinking subject and the object of thought. This dualism is nowhere more clearly evidenced than in language, which cannot be separated from the essential dualism of words and things. The words are not the things they stand for; they are signs— C. S. Peirce calls them *representamen*—that represent objects *in absentia* since any process of representation involves the removal of the object represented. The gap between sign and thing, the distance established through language (as a system of signs) implies both absence and presence of the thing—a dualism that inheres in language and, it appears, cannot be eradicated.

Language, therefore, is the Gordian knot. All promises to cut the latter have come up against the ineradicable fact that language stands for, or imitates, reality. The mimetic function of language implies a deformation of some preexisting reality and is consequently predicated upon difference. In fact, language *is* difference in more ways than has so far been suggested here through the dualistic approach (what, in short, has been presented as the schism between being and non-being). Linguistic structuralism has emphasized the primacy of difference over identity. Saussure's famous formula: "in language, there are only differences," expresses a radical view of the linguistic system in which the identification of the signs is based on their mutual exclusion. Each one is what the other is not. Saussure accepted no positive terms into the linguistic system, "only conceptual and phonic differences that derive from the system," he maintained.[1] This negative conception of language has considerably influenced postmodern philosophical thought, especially in France, as the work of Jacques Derrida or Gilles Deleuze, among others, amply shows.

Saussure's most innovative contentions, however, concerned

another variant of difference applied to two binary oppositions: the first one between *langue* and *parole,* language and speech acts, in which *langue* is seen but as a system of relations and oppositions whose elements must be defined in terms of difference, and *parole* as a nonfunctional manifestation of the above system in speech and writing. The other one refers to the two "faces" of the sign, the signifier and the signified, as closely connected to each other as "the recto and verso of a sheet of paper," Saussure wrote, yet as irremediably distant and different as those two.

While difference has now been recognized as one of the most basic constitutive principles of language as a system (*langue*), even in poststructuralist linguistics, it appears rather less performant as an operative device when it comes to analyzing speech acts or texts (*parole*). How is difference crucial, for instance, in the identification of "literary" texts, or, even more specifically, in distinguishing between prose and poetry? Such a question is considerably less scientific than, say, the Jakobsonian phonological analysis of a sentence, and yet needs some kind of systematic answer. In the case of poetry, it should be noted, contemporary theory has made substantial advances, to which the present volume would like to append its own modest contribution.

A last element adds to the complexity of theorizing on difference, and that is the temporality of being, of thought, and of discourse. A synchronic view has been taken of difference thus far. Yet the form in which the substance of being can be adequately appraised is temporal. One consequence of the Kantian criticism of Descartes' *cogito ergo sum* has been to reinscribe the determination of the subject and of its existence into the form of time. But time, as Deleuze, for instance, has shown in his essay *Différence et répétition,* also introduces in the conscious subject the awareness of its own division "before/after." And the presence of time in thought bears on the subject's own consciousness of himself (Deleuze refers to a "fissured I"—*Je fêlé*). Deleuze offers a radical conception of the "I" in the phrase "I think" by distinguishing a "phenomenal 'I'" (the subject that apprehends himself in time) and an "essential 'I'" (the one who spontaneously exerts the activity of thinking). According to him, then, what or who performs the thinking and says "I" is perceived as an "Other."

What is of import here is obviously the differentiation that time inserts into the development of thought and, by way of consequence, into discourse. The dialectic of the Same and the Other has repeatedly been expressed as a fundamental concern of philosophers from Spinoza, through Nietzsche and the motif of the "Eternal Return," down to this day. Binary combinations like identity/otherness, or unity/multiplicity, are expressions of ontological anxieties that overflow into the arts. The ideas of difference and of repetition inform the process of artistic representation as much as they supply material for philosophical inquiry.

Multiplicity and diversity, or resemblance and analogy, also belong to the realm of rhetoric and, through the centuries, also have sustained most theories of intepretation. What has changed in the modern era is that the compulsive quest for the Same, as the rock on which to build conceptual orders, has gradually shifted to the more unstable grounds of difference and indeterminacy, even though with an identical integrative purpose, which is now to demonstrate that difference itself may be used as a parameter of continuity and homogeneity in the apprehension and representation of the real—in other words, to restore the positiveness of difference.

Literary criticism has not escaped that shift. Without definitely denigrating the methodological models provided by structuralist linguistics, it has extended its areas of investigation into realms of meaning where difference—not to say "*différance*"—constantly pushes back the horizon of certitudes. The great epistemological turmoil in the last twenty years has yielded fascinating results, notably in the hands of deconstructionists who, as John Hillis Miller remarked, have attempted "to resist the totalizing and totalitarian tendencies of criticism."[2] Stimulating as their approach may have been, however, it may have failed to fully account for the role of difference in literary—especially poetic—texts; it may have failed, in fact, to perceive "the totalizing and totalitarian" forces at play in poetry as the very characters that make poetic discourse different from all other kinds of discourse.

The question yet to be answered, then, is what makes poetry "different?" Where should the line be drawn that divides poetry from nonpoetry? This kind of interrogation is not merely relevant to poetic texts: difference is the basis of all taxonomic processes. Yet it cannot serve as an exclusive criterion for classification. Difference is not a norm but an *écart* from the norm—no need to emphasize, here, how reductionist such a stance may become at the hands of the strictest normativists.

So the issue of difference in literature is inseparable from that of canonical texts and authors, and acquires obvious ideological overtones. But let's not anticipate. Suffice it to say, for the moment, that difference, as applied to the nature of literary texts, depends on some essential property they possess that, for want of a better term, we may call with Jakobson "literarity"—this being, as he wrote in *Questions de poétique,* "what makes of any given work a literary work."[3] As a subgenre of literature, poetry should receive a comparable treatment; so that the essence of poetry, the "poeticity" of poems should be what allows them to be recognized as such. Yet, to postulate a difference in the nature of texts does not give any particular clue as to the nature of the difference itself, especially as the boundaries between poetic and nonpoetic texts tend to become blurred today.[4]

Traditional rhetoric offered little ground for hesitation as it broke the poetic text down into a prosaic discursive core and an ornamentation that gave it its properly poetic character—what Paul Valéry called "a particular music" (*"une musique particulière"*). In this case, the model formula for poetry would be chiefly of a quantitative nature:

$$Poetry = prose + a + b + c$$

(a conception debunked by Roland Barthes in his *Le Degré zéro de l'écriture*). The difference marking poetry would thus be some added value to prose. The nature of that addition can be variously appraised according to whether the focus is set on the signifier or the signified sides of the linguistic sign. On one hand, formalists have insisted that verse derives from versification, that what "makes" poetry rests with all the additional formal constraints imposed on the signifier in poetic utterances. This view, which posits "poeticity" as a kind of over-codification of ordinary, prosaic, language has come under heavy critical fire from those who investigate the nature of poetry from the other angle, that of the signified. A poetic text is indeed a verbal construct that, as Jakobson intuited, displays an overload of sound games and word play; but it cannot be reduced to such articulations. Psychoanalytical criticism, in particular, has advised us to look for underlying meanings, for disguised messages beneath the surface of the text, variously accessible through the symbolic charge of the signifier or through its paragrammatic value. Over-codification here would concern significations, not just forms; yet poetry would remain quantitatively different from non-poetry. Also relevant to this critical line is the now fashionable polysemic approach which grounds its theoretical *raison d'être* on the assumption that a poetic text yields an infinity of possible combinations of significations, accessible through and opening the door to a corresponding infinity of readings. Multiplicity here is the criterion for the poetic, a sort of amplification of meaning that still depends on quantity.

But "poeticity," it appears, like "literarity" needs to be qualified as well as quantified, if only because qualitative traits, in objects and in concepts, are a source of differentiation. Truly enough, the very idea of "quality" is itself an arguable one. To observe "qualities" that would represent the essence of poetry requires, as Hume suggested, a combination of motivation and arbitrariness and a balance between them that would tilt towards the former. Quality, as founded on the repetition of the Same (same describable properties) is more unreliable than it seems. Phenomenologists have often demonstrated that repetition in the physical world is of a highly accidental nature. Randomness is the rule and regularity a subjective illusion. Jean Cohen, in his remarkable study on poetics, *Théorie de la poéticité,* reminds us that the ancient materialist philosophy was already very much antiqualitative, and quotes Democritus as observing: "The sweet and the sour, the hot and cold, the color of things are only matters of opinion; only atoms and the void are true."[5] A similar preponderance of indeterminacy was established by Galilean astronomy in the seventeenth century. Modern art's response to the contingencies and arbitrariness of the real was an attempt to abandon *mimèsis*—excessively dependent on its adherence to observable qualities—in favor of a perfectly formal construct whose rules would escape the arbitrary constraints of the natural world. And formalism was born of the necessary work on the signifier that such project entailed.

Quality, however, as a noticeable sign of recurrence and similarity (even sameness), is part of what makes poetic language different. One clear indication of this qualitative difference is to be found in the use of figures, of *écarts,* or deviations from linguistic norms that poetry involves. To the over-codification represented by the formula "Poetry = prose + X" we should substitute something like an *anti*-codification in which figurativeness would play a major part. The category of *écarts* would then include phonological, semantical, as well as syntactical deviations or dislocations. It remains that any sense of abnormality and *écart* presupposes the existence of infringeable norms, which, in turn, gives to the assessment of poetic difference a kind of radical touch that may serve only to marginalize poetry.

It should be observed that deviation from linguistic norms are not limited to poetry (child language, for instance, may be deviant without being necessarily poetic). So the problem of poeticity cannot be confined to the fact of respecting or not respecting the rules of language. What is at issue seems to be rather the *function* of deviational expression.

The function of poetic language, as we see it, is indeed to systematically infringe upon linguistic rules for the purpose of *intensification*. Jean Cohen, taking up Mallarmé's modernist views of what he called the "high language," very persuasively argues that the function of poetry is to provide a heightened expression of the real, to be what he charmingly calls "a verbal image of eternity,"[6] echoing Valéry's definition of poetic sensation as a "sensation of universes" ("*une sensation d'univers*").[7] The source of this intensification, we will recall, is to be found in the use of figures. Figures, as *écarts*, work in two different directions: first, Cohen suggests, they serve to liberate the poetic text from the norms of prosaic language essentially by blocking any possibility of negating its informative contents or syntactical structure. Poetry, he claims, is a language without negation, without contraries and, as such, aspires to a totalization of meaning. Poetry *is* totalitarian in the positive (nonpolitical) sense of the term. Figures play another part in the differentiation of poetry from nonpoetry: they drive poetic language away from the conceptual (as exemplified in scientific language) and towards the imaginary; they somehow manage to substitute images for concepts, thus affecting us more emotionally than an informative discourse. Poetic words are "felt," they are "more energized"—to borrow Pound's formula—than the words of prose. Poetry deals with "impressions;" to the difference of prose it does not seek to report on things, or on our consciousness of things, but to express how things "impress" us. Cries, exclamations, interjections, abundant as they are in poetry, are but marks of this drive towards an unencumbered expression of the original, powerful, emotions contained in the world of things.

To go back to what was said earlier, poetry mostly seeks to cancel the age-old dualism between subject and object, to cancel, so to say, the exteriority of things. Things in poetry are dynamically rendered, they leave the outer circle of existence that is not me to become absorbed into consciousness and become as many states of feeling (*états d'âme*). Two consequences: one is the importance of reader-response and how well-founded all the recent critical inquiries into this field have been. Another is the production of poetic texts and how poets perceive and conceive of their "own difference"—which is a question of appropriation and individuality. By extension, the idea of difference also colors the issue of cultural identity. Recent studies on "influence" have shown how relevant, not merely to the defining of poeticity but also to the writing impulse itself the idea of *écart* proves to be. Poets feel the weight of difference in their very need to exist as poets. In his now canonical *The Anxiety of Influence* Harold Bloom refers to the two constitutive elements of difference, identity and independence, which at once unite and disjoint, and remind us of the essentially paradoxical nature of difference. Bloom explains:

> "By 'poetic influence,' I do not mean the transmission of ideas and images from earlier to later poets ... Ideas and images belong to discursiveness and to history and are scarcely unique to poetry. Yet a poet's stance, his Word, his imaginative identity, his whole being, *must* be unique, or he will perish, as a poet, if ever even he has managed his rebirth into poetic incarnation. But this fundamental stance is as much also his precursor's as any man's fundamental nature is also his father's, however transformed."[8]

By turning the poetic activity into an ontological pursuit, Bloom is in fact reinserting the whole concept of influence—and of difference—into its temporal frame. This sense of continuity in attitudes towards the poetic material that Bloom refers to is inevitably historical and, in turn, closely related to the "fissure" (mentioned earlier) that time introduces into the conscious "I." As humans, poets must repeat and yet innovate, be the same and yet other in one breath. As poets, they must incorporate difference into the creative process. In a sort of double *mimèsis* they must work at a representation of difference within their own writing. Difference, then, becomes both a subject matter and a means for identification. William Carlos Williams hardly meant otherwise when he remarked, about the ur-poet of American letters: "The only way to be like Whitman is to write *unlike* Whitman. Do I expect to be a companion to Whitman by mimicking his manners ?"[9] Here Williams, not unintentionally, disincarnates Whitman into a kind of norm to be transgressed for the sake of differentiation. But the normative approach, useful as it might have been to help define what the "poetic" consists of, yields dubious results when it comes to measuring differences between poetic utterances, let alone whole corpuses, or the poets themselves as creators. If, to Mallarmé or Deleuze indifferently, poetry is an intensification of "ordinary" language, taken as a norm, then how (to go back to the above example) would Williams's poetry in some way "intensify" Whitman's? The question may not be as extravagant as it seems; intertextual studies have demonstrated to what extent poets "capitalize"— the verb is used here as blandly as the qualifier "totalitarian" was used earlier—on their predecessors' work, and, in their anxiety to be different, have striven to "go beyond" their literary fathers by experimenting on and with language.

Experimentation, in this case, is not motivated by an *a priori* refusal of the same, of imitation, of redundancy, as though difference was taken teleologically to be an objective or a mission, but by a desire to use difference as a working principle, to make it operational and instrumental in the production of poetic texts.

Critical readings of poetry, then, may be as diverse as their object of analysis, and the purpose of the present volume is to provide a testimony to how readers with a European academic background, or influenced by the European tradition of literary criticism, approach modern American poetry. Here are gathered a handful of case studies in poetic composition that may serve to shed light on the workings of difference in the emergence of that mark of the poetic we have called "poeticity;" which may also serve to question the reductive definition of poeticity that ancient rhetoricians described by the phrase *Nihil aliud quam fictio et rhetorica in musica posita*, ("Nothing but fiction and rhetoric put in music").

The term of "strategies" used to characterize the following essays on difference may itself seem reductive, but it has a double functional advantage: first, it draws the reader's attention back to the crafting of the poem and the intentionality of language. Poeticity is not the product of magic—though poetry may at first impress us as such—but the result of a deliberate manipulation of norms and codes. In this respect, writing poetry requires a high degree of arbitrariness, not just the kind inherent in the Saussurean linguistic sign but that which constantly tyrannizes signifiers to involve them into extraordinary combinations—a practice that became particularly productive with the Surrealists; André Breton once declared: "For me the most forceful images are those which express the highest level of arbitrariness." ("*Pour moi, l'image la plus forte est celle qui représente le degré d'arbitraire le plus élevé.*")[10] Second, it serves as an epistemological tool in the assessment of each poet's uniqueness and/or stance toward his material and toward other poets.

The canonical temptation to establish schools and traditions in art has been mostly censored by contemporary critics. Nowhere better than in America has modern poetry both been more prolific and better resisted classification—a resistance gleefully encouraged by Pound, for example, when in 1934 he scolded critics for their tendency to "coagulate their rather gelatinous attention on the *likeness*" between poets' works.[11] Focusing on difference may provide an alternative, especially if we postulate difference as constitutive of poetic composition. The question whether difference in critical evaluations of poetry—in other words difference as an epistemological strategy—is a sound heuristic instrument has not been discussed. It does not appear to be a precondition for the existence of this volume, yet may strike the reader as one of its possible extensions, and a valuable matter for further debate. The variety of critical opinions expressed in the following pages, at least, proves to offer a valid test of the diversity of poetic expression.

The first two essays develop their arguments on the basic assumption of the phenomenological difference between subject, object, and the world, to which should be added the distance introduced by figurativeness between the real and its mimetic representation (the poem) on one hand, and between the user of language and the linguistic construct on the other hand. Charles Altieri opens the debate with an analysis of "expressivity," or how the subject approaches the limits of lyrical form and tries to explore the uncharted territories beyond subjective expressivity. Altieri uses the study of two poems by W. B. Yeats, "Leda and the Swan" and "The Echo" as a case in point, to show the pain involved in the poet's realization of the mind's insufficiency in coping not only with the reality of an objective world but with the finality of the self's existence in that world. This is also the kind of anxious inquiry Gudrun Grabher finds at work in the poetry of A. R. Ammons and Jorie Graham: how to approach the essence of things, how even to be part of the objective world without relinquishing the status of subject? The answer, which owes much to Heideggerian existential philosophy, she finds to be empathy and the necessary blurring of the lines between subject and object.

Alain Suberchicot's concern is also with the lyrical "I" and its redefinition by Wallace Stevens. What he examines are the various alternatives Stevens experiments with, particularly by means of the seminal conflict between the immanent subject, the shifting tones of his voice within the poem and the metric constraints imposed on his discourse. That poetry is music played in different tones is a conventional metaphor that Stevens would hardly have rejected. But if signifiers "sing"—note that for Rimbaud poetry was "thought singing"—it is to more forcefully impress the receiver, to communicate ideas, to convey some sense of community. Pathos is deliberately directed towards the other, with the accepted risk of making the poetry appear histrionic. That "other" includes past others. And Alain Suberchicot investigates some of the ambiguous relations Stevens entertained with the traditions of American poetry. Such is, also, substantially the case of Anne Luyat-Moore's contribution, which surveys Stevens's participation in the 1943 *Entretiens de Pontigny* at Mount Holyoke College, his friendship with French philosopher Jean Wahl, and their differences on the relative positions of poetry and philosophy towards the real, under the looming shadows of T. S. Eliot and Bergson. The aborted controversy between Stevens and Wahl on the relevance of art to reality, as detailed by Anne Luyat-Moore, points to the issue of authority: authority of the text, of the poet, of the reader, of the critic. This is an inexhaustible source of differences since poetry as language of intensification also intensifies the critical discourse it instigates, and a source of confusion when it comes to assessing the truth of a poem, or approaching the truths of life through the poem. The critic faces the formidable challenge of "unlocking" the door to the impressions that the poet—to paraphrase Stevens—locked up in words. Poetry is not subsumed to conceptual clarity like prose. Mallarmé pleaded that "there must always be some enigma in poetry,"[12] elevating obscurity to the rank of a constitutive device of poeticity. Modern poetry has, in part, followed Mallarmé's demand, not merely on the formal level, through the play on signifiers, but, in a more sophisticated way, to try to express the poet's obscure and shifting modes of emotion, of affectivity. That what the reader reads in the poem should be different from the poet's original intent has been a matter of heated critical debate but seems hardly relevant here. What imports is to account for the affective intensity of the poem and how it impresses us. But, then, can we entirely evade the question of the poet's authority over his own text? Modern and postmodern poetics have sought to convince us of authorial deficiencies in this respect. Theories of influence, intertextuality, reader-response, etc., have cast doubt on the authority not just of the lyrical "I" but on the flesh and blood *maker* of the text. This is a process Axel Nesme sees illustrated by the intertextual relation which binds the work of Theodore Roethke to that of sixteenth-century philosopher-poet Sir John Davies. A similar concern is central to Massimo Bacigalupo's essay on Ezra Pound; yet, this time, the issue is that of the poet's own critical authority over his work. This applies all the better to Pound as his deliberately cryptic texts were but a devious way of establishing his dominance over his creation, and foiling beforehand all New Critical-type attempts at producing meaningful glosses about his poems. Although Bacigalupo never comes to such a conclusion, it seems that poetic truth is never available with the sort of scientific directness that, say, Newtonian physics provided. What modern poets have discovered is that the shining path to truth is more like some back-country road with twists and turns, that meanders through uncharted territory and where the only distinctive features are disturbances in its course, deviations akin to the turbulent *clinamens* at work in conventional physics. Could it be that only indeterminacy, or identifiable disturbances of meaning can lead us to the reality and the truth of facts? The question informs Charles Reznikoff's whole project when he wrote his *Testimony*. Geneviève Cohen-Cheminet tries, through the analysis of Reznikoff's narrative strategies, to find out how the poet strove to communicate the truth about the human condition in a way that might be expected of a court of law—something George Oppen, who was one of Reznikoff's friends, considered one of his major mistakes since, as he (Oppen) saw it, the truth about the human condition should be sought not in courts but in the streets. Few poets in this century, indeed, have taken to the streets for their inspiration, except perhaps those for whom the rhetorical presence of the Other led to an awareness of cultural (more than individual) differences and a desire to come to terms with them.

The way Nuyorican poet Tato Laviera chose is that of interlingual play. We often behave as though there existed only one universal language, our own, the mother (!) tongue, with words that express (unmistakably for us) the nature of our being. But for migrants, for people with multicultural backgrounds and experience, it is rather the differentiation between several languages that assumes real significance and supports the quest for identity. Laviera's bilingual poems, as Véronique Rauline points out, convey both a desire for blending and the conviction that linguistic divergence is creative and can open new fields of experiment for the poet. Such is also the case for Thomas Kinsella, the Irish expatriate, although his own bid for originality and anguished search for identity required some kind of affrontment with the language (which is that of the colonial power, England) and with the old masters of Irish literature (notably Yeats). Taffy Martin shows how deeply and carefully the sense of difference has been woven into his poems. Among the poets studied here probably no one has made such an extensive use of difference as a conscious strategy for poetic composition.

There is no way for the poet, nor for us, to ignore the fact that "the difference is part of the thing itself," as French philosopher Michel Serres, who was also a scientist by training, observes. On the perception of difference depends our sense of identity; on the conceptualization of difference depends the manner in which we identify the products of our imagination. Yet the most fascinating property of difference is its dynamism, how it spawns an infinity of deriving differences in a cascade of echoing and dependent effects. For that reason, difference as a phenomeno-logical trait of poetry is likely to inspire and generate a profusion of debates on the nature of poetic composition and of poeticity. To serve as introduction, example and stimulus for such discussions is admittedly both the justification and the objective of the following essays.

Notes

1. F. de Saussure, *Cours de linguistique générale* (Paris: Payot, 1968), 166. (my translation).
2. Quoted in Harold Bloom et al., *Deconstruction and Criticism* (New York: Continuum, 1979), 252.
3. Roman Jakobson, *Questions de poétique* (Paris: Seuil, 1976), 15.
4. Jean Cohen, in *Théorie de la poéticité* (Paris: José Corti, 1995), points to the fact that contemporary philosophy and criticism make wide use of figu-rative language while still announcing their definite scientific purpose; he takes Foucault and Barthes as significant examples (13–14).
5. Quoted in Cohen, *Théorie,* 204.
6. Cohen, *Théorie,* 214.
7. Paul Valéry, *"Propos sur la poésie,"* in *Oeuvres complètes,* vol. 1 (Paris: Gallimard, 1959), 1363.
8. Harold Bloom, *The Anxiety of Influence,* (New York: Oxford University Press, 1973), 71.
9. William Carlos Williams, "America, Whitman, and the Art of Poetry," *Poetry Journal* (November 1917): 31.
10. Quoted in Jean Cohen, *Théorie,* 86.
11. The poets concerned here were William Carlos Williams and George Oppen. Ezra Pound, Preface to *Discrete Series* (New York: The Objectivist Press, 1934), v.
12. Stéphane Mallarmé, *"Je disais quelquefois ...,"* in *Oeuvres complètes,* vol. 1 (Paris: Gallimard, 1949), 365.

Lyric Form and Lyric Force: Yeats and the Limits of the Expressivist Tradition

Charles Altieri

I WILL BEGIN WITH AN OLD-FASHIONED CLOSE READING, THEN TRY TO show how that practice helps us handle two relatively new fashions. I want to use Yeats as a representative for modernism's version of what we now take as a postmodern project of setting lyrical force against lyrical form, so that the undoing of form becomes the poem's basic means of bringing into the open what its culture represses or ignores. I also want to show how Yeats's efforts in this regard require recasting models of agency shaped initially by the tradition of romantic expressivism. One can trace these changes because contemporary criticism has done a good job of making clear how this expressivist tradition provided alternatives to Enlightenment ideals of representation and Enlightenment versions of freedom and judgment. But this work has tended to equate expressivism with a humanist focus on the self-reflexive capacities of individual subjects that does not do full justice to the intense efforts of some modernists to escape that way of idealizing human powers by setting themselves against both the Enlightenment and its romantic antagonists.

Close reading becomes central because it enables us to see how lyric poetry can take on the philosophical force to modify our understanding of what is at stake in these confrontations. Therefore I turn to Yeats's "Leda and the Swan" because that poem provides the most succinct rendering I know of the salient issues.[1] As you read the poem, ask why it must end in a question and how the syntax works to flesh out a possible way of answering that question:

> A sudden blow: the great wings beating still
> Above the staggering girl, her thighs caressed
> By the dark webs, her nape caught in his bill,
> He holds her helpless breast upon his breast.

How can those terrified vague fingers push
The feathered glory from her loosening thighs?
And how can body, laid in that white rush,
But feel the strange heart beating where it lies?

A shudder in the loins engenders there
The broken wall, the burning roof and tower
And Agamemnon dead.
      Being so caught up,
So mastered by the brute blood of the air,
Did she put on his knowledge with his power
Before the indifferent beak could let her drop?[2]

It is by now a commonplace to point out how the content of
this poem strains against the sonnet form. Even the opening
absolute participial construction posits a sense of immediacy
so consuming that it seems to demand a challenge to syntactic
coherence. And similar pressures set the sonnet's sextet in
sharp opposition to the resolving roles tradition assigns it. Here
the indicative statements only repeat the sense of disaster, this
time in a string of metonymies indicating the tragic consequences of the rape. It seems, then, as if the sonnet can no
longer provide the kind of argument that in Shakespeare and in
Milton would account for the pressures that the poem is
responding to and would dialectically restore at least the appearance of discursive coherence. Instead, where we expect argument to begin we get only these metonyms and, in reaction, an
abrupt return to the original event, as if the effort to imagine
history could not get past the original violence that set it in
motion. If there is to be any mastery on the part of the witnessing consciousness, it will have to emerge from within the
replaying of trauma rather than in any thematic recasting of it.
 The poem uses two basic syntactic devices in order to focus
its response to that challenge. First, the final lines so strongly
echo the participial structure of the opening that we are invited
to reflect on how the two relate to each other. The initial participial construction offers a nominative absolute followed by ge-
rundive present participles that cannot be placed in direct
syntactic relation with any of the main grammatical units of the
sentence registering the rape. It seems as if the emergence of
this god requires our working through several kinds of contingency, only to be forced to recognize that this mode of power
need not depend on any of our qualifiers for his existence. In-

stead, divinity may simply be force capable of generating such syntactic diffusiveness.

By the end of the poem, it seems as if another relation to participles becomes possible, this time in a string of past participles that can serve as modifiers of the subject in the final main clause. Indeed, one might say that the very process of modification provides the only evidence we have of any cogent interpretive stance achieved by the responding consciousness; so it is tempting to take the work of modification as the poem's basic answer to its own question about knowledge and power. There clearly cannot be any direct thematic answer to the question, since such an answer would depend on identifying with Leda at depths that probably she could not reach herself. And one would then have to have a language capable of delineating what one discovered, as if one were capable of understanding what terms like "knowledge" and "power" and, perhaps most important, "could" mean to a god. Yet even without that direct answer, the poem suggests there can be an intensity of questioning that becomes a kind of answer in its own right, since it enables the speaking voice to place disruptive energies within a cogent syntactic structure. So we are led to wonder if knowledge can be correlated with such power without deluding itself into thinking it can propose satisfying interpretations for the unsettling forces that constitute historical events.

To flesh out this line of thinking, we must turn to the second set of foregrounded syntactic relations in the poem, its uses of the interrogative. The second quatrain offers the first set of interrogatives. Their task is to allow some space for the powers of consciousness within an event dominated by the god's refusal to be bound by any human standards or rationales. Unable to make sense of the god, the poem tries questions as its mode of at least reaching out to what torments Leda in her confrontation with the divine presence. Questions become vehicles for exploring the possibility of making identifications—initially with Leda's efforts to resist, then, more intensely, with the beating of her heart, that is with the most intimate site where she was actually connected to that divine strangeness.

The metonymy of the heart soon gives way to a more general string of metonymies tracing the consequences of this rape. Then, to get beyond a world reduced to such metonymies, the poem turns once more to the interrogative. But now the interrogatives are focused less on emotional identification than they are on developing some mode of consciousness that can register not only the effect of the rape on Leda but also its impact on others because of its status as a historical event. Once we understand the consequences of the rape we all become Zeus's victims, and, more importantly, the central drama ceases to be a matter only of what the event felt like. Now we need to understand power in a way that engages the causal force it brings to bear on all of human history.

But in order to engage that level of trauma, such knowledge must allow us to transcend the mere witnessing position in which both Leda and the speaking consciousness find themselves—witnesses are only victims and cannot comprehend what victimizes them. We must develop a level of comprehension that can raise witnessing to a state where it enables us also to try out identifications with the divine force entering our history. Yeats manages to open a way for that parallel by the brilliant move of projecting something beyond the god, some force determining whether the "indifferent beak could let her drop." Now, even the god has a passive dimension that we may be able to share, as if by fully recognizing our own absolute limitations we could also imagine the strange combination of activity and passivity fundamental to the god's entering the causal forces that shape history.

The best way to elaborate the implications of the poem's final question is to return to the theme of modification. The syntax of this last stanza suggests that the interrogative mode itself offers a vehicle for appreciating the complex interrelations among Leda's victim status, the god's power, and whatever dictates the "could" to that power.[3] The interrogative preserves the absolute strangeness of this incarnation, but it also provides a means of identifying with those who must encounter that strangeness—both as Leda does and as Zeus eventually does. The questioning itself may constitute the version of knowledge best suited to engage fully what living in history entails: appreciating the full plight of those Leda comes to represent requires this constant effort to identify with suffering that cannot be described by any positive knowledge without being displaced into something it is not. And yet such questioning need not reduce us to Leda's victim status. Questioning also becomes a means of rivaling the god because the syntax of questioning can be transformed simply by its intensity into the syntax of exclamation.

The internal patterning we have been tracing provides precisely that intensity, so that the poem's structuring of syntax comes to represent both the unmaking and the remaking of the power of lyric forms. Sonnet order must be submitted to the absoluteness of events. But the transgression of form opens the possibility of another model for comprehending the force of events. The intense identification that questioning can establish becomes in its own gathering and self-grounding power, the only mode of knowledge that history's victims *could* achieve.

So much for close reading. That approach can elaborate ideas, but it cannot in itself show why they matter. To do that, I will shift from being absorbed by a particular to quite loose and quick generalizations, since these seem to me the only way within a single essay to show how Yeats's poem can be said to participate in one crucial cultural struggle basic to modernist poetry and now fundamental to poststructuralist theory. This struggle is to find ways of getting free of the visions of expressive agency put in place by German idealism and, in the arts, by romanticism, while continuing to explore the ways in which that vision opens alternatives to Enlightenment ideals of method and definitions of agency in terms of empirical interests and practical judgments. What must be rejected is the tendency to make the empirical subject both the locus of the forces driving expressions and the telos for whatever articulation we can give to those forces.

Were Yeats only a last romantic he would concentrate on Leda's struggle to articulate her own plight, and in the process forge an identity for herself. If Wordsworth or even Arnold were to deal with Leda's situation, they would cast Leda as the questioner hoping to make the questions a vehicle for articulating an increasingly more intricate understanding of her own identity within her cultural setting. And on the basis of such articulation she could represent herself as somehow taking responsibility for her fate. However, Yeats never lets her, or the witnessing consciousness, take up an empirical situation for the self or get beyond the interrogative. This means that insofar as his poem can claim any kind of exemplary status, it does not idealize any commitment to the individual psyche or even any dialectical process for raising such a psyche to "higher," more comprehensive levels of consciousness. All he offers is this presentation of questioning as consciousness's most capable vehicle for engaging the forces that work their way to expression through us. Therefore we need now to attempt to understand why he puts on himself such limitations and what one can claim are the positive dimensions of accepting those limitations as preconditions for imaginative work. In pursuing this question, we will see Yeats's critique of romantic expressivism bringing him quite close to fundamental poststructural concerns, but he does so in order to suggest an alternative model for how experiments in lyric form can define possible sites of subjective agency.

I can generalize so glibly about romantic expressivism because the work of Charles Taylor, Northrop Frye, and Gilles Deleuze provides a clear understanding of how German idealism and the romantic movement opened a cultural dispensation sharply at odds with dominant Enlightenment attitudes.[4] Through their work, we can realize how thoroughly romanticism not only resisted the basic concepts of Enlightenment rationality but also fostered different prevailing models for how ideas can be developed, interrelated, and tested, since its expressivist thinking takes its basic logic from the arts rather than from an idealized picture of scientific inquiry.

These thinkers recognize the diversity within idealist and romantic thinking. But they also locate a central shared concern that comes to the foreground when we focus on how they all cast themselves as opposing Enlightenment rationality because of what seemed an inescapable dilemma confronting its accounts of subjective agency. On the one hand, the Enlightenment cultivated individual self-legislation working itself free of all external determinants imposed by superstition and by social pressures. On the other hand, when Enlightenment thinkers tried to account for human actions, they saw no alternative to seeking explanations for subjective events that were no different in principle from the modes of explanation employed in the sciences. As Kant saw clearly, what the Enlightenment freed as the subject of choice it also tried to recontain as the object of a knowledge incompatible with the indeterminacies and models of legislative power necessary for any strong sense of subjective agency.

Going back to neo-Platonic thought, expressivist theory tried instead to redefine the relation between subject and object. Subjects were not agents exercising a purely individual will that was both opposed to the world of objects and yet bound to the same kinds of explanations used for objects. Freedom was less a state of being than a quality of lives that could be won by managing to make individual orientations articulate so that agents could then take responsibility for them. As Taylor puts it, expression in this strong sense consists in "clarification of meaning" that is also "the clarification of purpose" (*Hegel* 18). By expressing myself I also create a self to which I can refer my decisions—defining a self is inseparable from having articulate moral grounds, and it enables us to give consistency to those evaluations that we make on the basis of principle while keeping principle grounded in a particular history. Therefore one can say that in taking such responsibility agents join subjective individuality with a set of predicates that can be treated as giving that agent existence as an object for others, so long as one is also willing to locate that objectivity in relation to how agents came to represent the relation between reasons, desires, and patterns of experience forming the individual life. Expressions could not be understood, nor responsibility made intelligible, so long as knowledge required the impersonal and impartial procedures employed in the sciences.

For Kant, this synthesis of determination and identification derived from that agent's taking the stance of a self-legislating spirit capable of affirming its own lawfulness. But that same legislative relation to an objective process of self-determination could also be imagined taking place within an individual creative process. A poet like Wordsworth could explain his sense of his own freedom by relying on an autobiographical account defining both the forces shaping his life and his capacities to give eloquent realization to those forces. In the expressive process, Wordsworth not only gained greater clarity about his fealties and responsibilities, he also showed how one could embrace them as defining his own sense of identity. We know a person by recognizing how they give form to content and hence take responsibility for what their upbringing gives them.

Taylor shows that these shifts from Enlightenment priorities produced four new cultural aspirations, aspirations that we can now see as also forming the social agenda of most significant art since Romanticism (23–29). There emerged "a passionate demand for unity and wholeness," directed both towards an acute awareness of the various dichotomies haunting agents' self-representations and towards an increasing sense of alienation from those resources in nature that might heal those dichotomies. Correlatively, the emphasis on freedom as self-expression required reshaping notions of cultural evil in order to emphasize social blocks to "authentic self-expression" and to invent alternative forms of social life. Third, since freedom could no longer be a matter simply of stating preferences, ideals of expressive agency had to be located within the experience of creative forces that, when brought to expression, might ally persons with grounds for values more comprehensive than anything the individual, by relying only on preferences and practical judgments, might construct. Finally, this suspicion of pure individualism generated a desire for union with other men based on the idea that citizens shape the life of the polis and find themselves expressed within it: the fullest freedom becomes the realization of what is potentially collective in that shaping spirit.

Taylor's account makes very good sense as a historical analysis, but I fear that his own thinking about expression gets drawn problematically within this historical orbit in ways that help us understand why modernist artists and poststructural theorists are so vigilant in expunging their own inclinations towards romantic values. Any theory of expression must establish what kind of signs bear expressive force, and, more importantly, it must say what the marks of expressive force are expressions of: what is it that elicits the expressive activity (which can be either the revealing of something, as symptoms do, or the active composing of new significance), and how can one attribute psychological and ethical import to the relation between the articulation and the force it mediates. Taylor, in essence, handles both the question of force and the question of import in terms of the dynamics of subjective agency. While constantly flirting with and fighting off a simple idealization of authenticity, he attributes that force driving expressive activity to inchoate factors within a person's life history that the agent wants to clarify and take responsibility for. So the telos of expressive activity then involves a complex of values around notions of knowledge, responsibility and bonds to the expressive structures that come to elicit identifications with larger communities.

Taylor's investments are by no means trivial. They sustain and are sustained by substantial traditions and they allow cogent teleologies for self-interests and for communal life. However, they also bind him to linking expression with narrative and, more generally, they impose a model of human control and self-possession that risks losing the deeper sources of expressive energies, which may have the hold they do on us precisely because they cannot be contained within our efforts at articulation or, more interestingly, because what articulation we can give them challenges our own idealizations of subjective power and of social bonds based on mutual efforts at self-clarification. (Hegel himself was quite aware of that tendency within expressivist

labor because only such alienation could keep vital the difference between Spirit and those empirical agents who manifest
its emerging aspects.)

One could go on to distinguish two basic ways in which modernism carried out this critique of romantic expressivism. I will
mention only the first way here because it is the central concern
of my *Painterly Abstraction in Modernist American Poetry.* In
that book, I concentrate on how modernist painting and modernist poetry attempt to remake constructive agency by focusing
on aspects of expressive force that cannot be handled if we imagine agency along romantic terms, but instead require developing
constructivist principles that treat agency as something defined
by the intricate syntax of works of art. Instead of linking the
imagination with the autobiographical labor of giving definition
and representative force to particular life histories and patterns
of organizing experience, this art and this poetry turned instead
to what Wilhelm Worringer called the demonic and daimonic
aspects of experience that could not be captured within any
received notion of representation.

From this perspective, the forces seeking expression cannot
be adequately grasped if we relate them only to stories of persons
managing to bring into self-conscious narratives what had been
blocked or unrealized. Instead, modernist writers found their
initial interest in romantic versions of personal expression leading them to aspects of force so intimate, so embedded in our
desires and our actions, that they could no longer be attributed
to specific life histories. Instead, the imperatives to expression
must be located in transpersonal factors that, for art, require
either the abstract principles of structure and balance that fasci-
nated artists like Mondrian, or the pure willfulness of a Picasso
or, quite differently, a Duchamp, who ends up playing with and
upon the autobiographical impulse. Similarly, modernist writers
would turn to processes of feeling, knowing, and making that
had to be seen as transpersonal because their power and shape
clearly could not be derived from any biographical account of
specific agents. Precisely because the individual cannot be the
source of such energies and form, one might be able to make the
exploration of expressive forces also an exploration of possible
imperatives calling for collective actions and forging social
bonds.

The second way of asking what expressions are expression of
shifts the focus from discovering possible imperatives within
abstract forms to exploring values that might emerge if artists

concentrate on undoing the forms by which cultural life contains those forces seeking expression. From this perspective,
best articulated in Hegel's remarkable chapter on force, one can
claim that the only way to register the full impact of those impulses seeking expression is to refuse to rest in any particular
proposed realization of them. Force remains active as force only
to the degree that it cannot be subsumed under concepts or
appropriated by individual wills to expressive power. Hence in
Yeats, the encounter with the god does not lead to any positive
or determined knowledge, except insofar as it marks the limitations of any assertion and any traditional ideal of lyric closure.
Speaking in more general terms, we might say that postromantic
versions of expressivism must deal continually with the possibility that the basic forces driving our efforts at expression must
be phenomena we know best only by distorting least. And that
means committing the arts to the constant unrealizing of determinate forms. Art can hope to embody this force, but we cannot
assume that consciousness can successfully translate such embodiment into the symbolic register where predicates can then
be attached to what gets expressed.

By this logic, the central task of artistic experiment becomes
finding ways to generate intricate self-reflexive processes at least
as attentive to the margins of sense and resistances to determination as it is to those moments when it can claim to offer
positive articulations of what compels it. This opens art to a
complex ironic play with its genetic conditions and, at the other
pole, it makes it possible to explore modes of idealization that
are not based on the symbolic order, and hence not dependent
on the narratives selves tell about each other. Those moments
where the expressive energies of self seem somehow directly
connected to certain generative forces can take the form of Kristeva's *chora,* or, more complexly, of the *jouissance* that Lacan
came increasingly to project as the closest consciousness comes
to a reality it must repress in order to maintain any representation of itself.

Correlatively, once the force driving expressions is set in irreducible tension with our efforts at self-articulation, we must
begin to imagine imperatives to expression that also link us to
collective modes of life without relying on the problematic approach to sociality we find in Taylor's work. Taylor's expressivism treats an agent's political filiations as depending on two
aspects of self-reflection: participating in a collective process can
produce a mode of intelligibility about the shape and ends of

the social order that extends personal articulations into a larger
theater so that otherwise different subjects can identify as one;
and once we understand how collective identities are established, we have a strong case for arguing that those identities
are to be valued above the individualism they transcend. But
once the force seeking expression is identified with the collective, the possibility of transcending the individual becomes inseparable from the danger of denying the individual the power
or the right to differ substantially from the collective's self-
interpretation. Then to express the self is only to enter more
deeply into modes of subjection imposed by some collective order. So if we are to escape that impasse, we must define sociality
in terms that depend less on self-reflection about origins, and
more on how the process of expression creates imaginative sites
for the agents to explore on their own terms. Then sociality will
consist not in what we can say about defined collective identities,
but in the structure of relations that become visible because a
new strong particular has entered the social space. The particular makes dynamic certain attributes, as if they were edges
within the scene whose boundaries also had to be considered
anew: what can limit or oppose this expression; what binary
oppositions does it engender and clarify; or what alternative sets
of relations open so that old binaries, like the one between
knowledge and power, no longer seem quite appropriate for ne-
gotiating this new territory?

Setting a radical notion of expressive force against a romantic
ideal of making individual being increasingly articulate is easy
to oversimplify or distort. Most surrealist art and theory, for
example, recognizes the danger of making the self-reflexive
agent the principle by which the basic forces seeking expression
are realized. But it then tends to theorize an alternative set
of active forces that are as thematizable by a rhetoric of the
unconscious as romantic subjectivity is by idealizations of a dialectical process. Poststructural theory offers a more complex and
suggestive undoing of romantic expressivity in the name of
forces that cannot be brought under dialectical strategies. But
it is tempting to concentrate only on those aspects of the expressive forces which can be said to elude all efforts at articulation,
so all we can do is track the singular signature they elicit, or
deconstruct all the categories that get imposed on them. While
such moves have considerable philosophical warrant, they may
narrow too drastically what can go on in the kind of experiments

that we saw Yeats exploring. Ironically, poststructuralist literary criticism tends to ignore the brilliant recuperative aspects of Derrida's deconstructive analyses of concepts like "spirit" and the blindness that is fundamental to self-portraiture.

Jean-Luc Nancy's recent work provides something very close to an exemplary poststructural treatment of those aspects of expressivity that cannot be contained within idealized, dialectical versions of self-identity, in ways that also make clear the dangers that I see in that enterprise. Because the very notion of subject carries implications allied with Hegel's notion of an entity "'which is capable of maintaining within itself its own contradiction,'" Nancy seeks a way of getting outside the entire structure of idealizations deriving from idealist thought. So he asks us to imagine not who we are as subjects, but what sense we can give to the question "who comes after the subject." This "who" leads us to the many aspects of psychic life which cannot be gathered within the single perspective required to posit a distinct self-gathering subject—ranging from the impulses that lead us to focus our attention on specific phenomena to the contradictory pulls that become manifest in our actions. If we are to speak positively about subjective agency at all, we must base our value claims on what we can make emerge in our deconstructing the very concept of "subject." And then we find ourselves encountering "not the subject of existence but the existence-subject: that to which one can no longer allot the grammar of the subject, nor, therefore, to be clear, allot the word 'subject.'"[5] Expressivity becomes a version of Yeatsian questioning. For if we can look beyond the subject, the process of coming, in all its senses, takes the place of the structuring force of dialectic. Subjectivity is not a content but a certain kind of event, of emergence, that we can project as "the coming into space of a time, in a spacing that allows that something come into presence, in a unique time that engenders itself in this point in space, as its spacing" (7).

Nancy's formula directly takes on the Enlightenment tendency to treat the subject as if it could become an object for knowledge. Instead, we get a version of existentialism that locates singularity not in some mysterious and unanchored choosing but in the play of *jouissance* within constantly shifting frameworks. However, the model of spacing which Nancy uses to capture the force of this *jouissance* also carries a severe limitation. It has trouble handling the kind of concentrated negativity that we saw in Yeats's poem because that depends on an

intensity of focus and an effort at identification difficult to corre-
late with the fluidity and multiplicity inherent in the idealization of coming as a model for singular action. Yeats shows that
there can be resistance to romantic ideals that need not renounce structure or sustained duration or even a deep sense of
enduring responsibility. While poststructural literary criticism
offers a virtual Kama Sutra of ways of coming, it has no language
whatsoever for discussing how authors arrive at purposes or how
we might interpret, assess, and use those purposes. All value
resides in the working of singularities as they resist the categori-
zations that attempt to fix them in formulated phrases, so that
model does not allow us to distinguish between deconstructing
the subject and locating through deconstruction a sense of sublime individual powers that we can respond to even though we
cannot describe how they work.

I dwell on Nancy in order to support the suggestion that
twentieth-century poets' struggles against the dialectical forms
basic to romantic expressivism lead to different imaginative
strategies than those stressed within poststructuralism, while at
the same time sharing its basic resistances to categorical and to
autobiographical modes of interpreting the force within events.
Let me now try to secure that claim by closing with an analysis
of one more poem by Yeats, "Man and Echo." There is no richer
critique of romantic dialectics, and perhaps no more suggestive
account of what we gain by carrying out that critique with terms
less in bondage to the history of philosophy than those adapted
by Nancy and most poststructural theory.
    Yeats opens the poem by presenting himself as descending to
the bottom of a pit, which offers a private, unembarrassing place
to confront the fact that "All that I have said and done . . . turns
into a question":

> Did that play of mine send out
> certain men the English shot?
> Did words of mine put too great strain
> On that woman's reeling brain?
> Could my spoken words have checked
> That whereby a house lay wrecked?
> And all seems evil till I
> Sleepless would lie down and die.[6]

But the cave will not quite countenance such self-importance.
It echoes the last phrase, "lie down and die," and in so doing

defines for the speaker an imperative implicit in the perspective
he is taking. In one sense that imperative is only an echo, only
a trick of nature, yet it also suggests how tenuous it is to seek
meaning for the self in terms of the narrative details of a life:
one cannot find in that locale any principle capable of resisting
or dignifying the weariness and the self-critical lucidity of a body
no longer quite able to generate illusions about its own powers.
Nature's power to inflict death proves more compelling than the
spirit's efforts to establish an intelligible substance for itself.

But this doubling afforded by the echo's negation does push
the mind to a new beginning in the poem's second section, as
if self-objectification through the echo inaugurated a classical
dialectical process:

> That were to shirk
> The spiritual intellect's great work,
> And shirk it in vain. There is no release
> In a bodkin or disease,
> Nor can there be work so great
> As that which cleans man's dirty slate . . .

Now the speaker can look back to appreciate how the body's
stupidity provided some protection against such truths,

> But body gone he sleeps no more,
> And till his intellect grows sure
> That all's arranged in one clear view,
> Pursues the thoughts that I pursue,
> Then stands in judgment on his soul.
> And, all work done, dismisses all
> Out of intellect and sight
> And sinks at last into the night.

And now when the echo enters, repeating the phrase, "Into the
night," it seems as if the forces that sponsor it have become
somewhat more sympathetic to his plight, even though they still
refuse to be seduced by Yeats's efforts to pretend that consciousness can generate an intricate dialectic capable of dispelling the
otherness with which mortality confronts it.

Not even this apparent sympathy will win for the echo the
power to utter the last word, however. Yeats can still turn to the
strategies of questioning that proved so useful in "Leda and the
Swan." At least then one can directly address the deconstructive
force of the echo effect:

> O Rocky Voice,
> Shall we in that great night rejoice?
> What do we know but that we face
> One another in this place?
> But hush, for I have lost the theme,
> Its joy or night seem but a dream;
> Up there some hawk or owl has struck,
> Dropping out of sky or rock,
> As stricken rabbit is crying out,
> And its cry distracts my thought.

Yeats hopes that the intensity of questioning will provide an alternative mode of self-possession. If one cannot understand mortality or compose roles establishing a tragic dignity, one can hope that fully participating imaginatively in the resulting disenfranchisement might provide an alternative locus of spiritualization, just as hatred of God can be envisioned as generating an intensity and comprehensiveness that brings the soul to God. Yet here Yeats cannot be content even with that means of recuperating faith in some kind of compositional power. So the mode of questioning too must be deconstructed, as if even it continued to satisfy humanist illusions.

Where else can the poet turn? This poem offers as the beginning of a possible answer the suggestion that the cry of the rabbit offers an expressive voice giving some kind of meaning to the pain and spacing for the subject even as it loses its faith in dialectical strategies and in mythological projections allowing human analogues with the gods. Presenting a Yeatsian version of the "chorister whose c preceded the choir" in the last poem of Stevens's *Collected Poems*,[7] this cry offers a note of reality that by contrast exposes all the poet's spiritual work as deeply pervaded by illusion. Yet the illusion is not simply something to be cast aside. A minimalist version of the old dialectic returns, only now without any claims about the integrative powers of the empirical subject. As in Wittgenstein's reminder that we need shadows in order to recognize what serves as light, it takes the entire process of the poem for us to be able to appreciate everything that this cry contains while not reintroducing humanistic consolations it will not sanction.

Now we find ourselves confronting modernism's version of the basic problem facing all deconstructive strategies: how do we formulate within language what reveals to us the inherent limitations in the languages we must use and the models of understanding we must rely upon? In what ways can we give positive content to such negative work without immediately reproducing the problems of representation or settling for vague pieties about the sublime? Obviously, there cannot be any direct answer to such questions that does not presuppose precisely what is being problematized, but we can try to align ourselves with the indirect strategies that works of art invite us to explore. In this case, Yeats calls attention to a question which makes it possible to recast the entire drama: why at the end is there no longer any echo? One could imagine Ovid extending the game by having the echo repeat the phrase "my thought," or even repeat the more enticing because utterly self-contradictory phrase (for an echo) "distracts my thought." But Yeats seems to think more is accomplished by suggesting that the poem has brought us to a point where the echo is either impossible or unnecessary. Once we begin to ask why that is the case we realize that there cannot be a significant echo of such distracted thoughts, since they have none of the unacknowledged materiality that haunts the conclusion of the other two stanzas. And, more importantly, it may be the case that the poem no longer needs an echo because now the repeated references to the rabbit's cry can suffice to double the poet's voice and to signify a different version of its irreducible submission to what it cannot control.

Once the echo is banished, so too is the set of dualisms that haunted the poem. Without echoes there need be no sharp gulf between the poet's reflective consciousness and the mortality that resists and embarrasses it. Reduced to distracted thought, the poet is no longer in the position of seeking supplements which provide a measure of self-importance at the cost of intensifying his division from the necessities of his corporeal nature. Instead, the pure event of the rabbit's cry provides precisely the voice the speaker needs to express what he represses—the fact that this entire effort at dialectic may be reducible to this pure cry, to a level of experience where even questions impose too much human shape to register the depth of pain that his mortality now imposes. Only by working against all human expressive forms does he realize the elemental pain that has been demanding expression all along.

And what an expression it becomes! If the cry can replace the echo, there need no longer be a problematic hope that the intricate evasions of dialectic can handle the gulf between subject and object, theatricalized self and patheticized nature. Unable to call upon dialectic, poetry learns to function by the intricate but uncontrollable work of exploring how affective equations

unfold in various dimensions. In this contingency, subjectivity
empties itself out, yet finds within its own consciousness of loss
its deepest affinity with everything that must live only as flesh.
The undoing of form itself is necessary to discover what it is
that makes us seek form in the first place.

Yeats himself uses this occasion to supplement the echo that
the cave produces by an echo effect emerging from his own investments as a lyric poet. For the momentary identification with
the rabbit's cry brings him back to his "The Sad Shepherd," the
second poem in his *Collected Poems,* where the poet ends up
reduced to speaking his sorrows to an echoing shell:

> But the sad dweller by the sea-ways lone
> Changed all he sang to inarticulate moan
> Among her wildering whirls, forgetting him.

(9)

But by 1938 the echoing has become a means of remembering,
not of forgetting. For the speaker is no longer positioned as part
of this dualistic opposition between subjective pain and self-
fascinating natural plenitude. The very process of emptying
himself seems to release him from demanding the kind of meanings which ultimately destabilize what they would secure. Opt-
ing for pure contingency, his new space opens a sense of time
that is not regret and of memory that is not torn by guilt.

Yeats gathers all these themes for one complex synthetic yet
depersonalized act by relying on one more echo, this time invok-
ing the first poem of his last published volume:

> The gyres! The gyres! Old Rocky Face look forth;
> Things thought too long can be no longer thought
> For beauty dies of beauty, worth of worth . . .
>
> In ancient tombs I sighed, but not again;
> What matter? Out of cavern comes a voice
> And all it knows is that one word 'Rejoice.'

(293)

If the cry replaces the echo, perhaps it also serves as the poet's
own secular analogue to this imperative spoken by the rocky
voice. For the sequence that prepares Yeats to hear in the rabbit's
cry whatever can stop the echoing may also provide a means of
turning distraction itself into a profound mode of affirmatively
identifying with that mortality. Then this cry becomes insepa-

rable from the only prayer available to Yeats: that the cry itself be so rammed with consciousness that it suffices at once to express both the spirit's insufficiency and its capacity to accept all that it cannot be because that acceptance gives it a way of establishing what the poet can still claim as his available powers. The most intimate level of affirming the self requires the most general awareness of how this decentering of the ego's demands intensifies consciousness's engagement in the transpersonal fatalities that bind thinking to being.

Notes

1. For a good theoretical account of "event" in the strong sense of singular moment that demands change in our relations to received ideas, see John Rajchman, *Philosophical Events* (New York: Columbia University Press, 1991). I should also note that a shorter version of this essay was given as a talk in a conference on lyric form directed by Pierre Lagayette and sponsored by the University of Paris 10, Nanterre.

2. Yeats, *The Poems of W.B. Yeats,* edited by Richard J. Finneran (New York: Macmillan, 1983), 214–15. I use a similar reading of this poem for quite different purposes in my "The Values of Articulation: Aesthetics After the Aesthetic Ideology," forthcoming in a collection of essays edited by Richard Eldridge (New York: Cambridge University Press).

3. We might also look at the theme of questioning as it gets played out in Yeats's "Supernatural Songs," where the intensity of questioning itself becomes as close as the soul can get to self-possession and intensity it postulates in God, and then opposes because it cannot share in God's power of making energies determinate.

4. I will base this particular account on Taylor's *Hegel* (Cambridge: Cambridge University Press, 1985), 10–46. Taylor is more elaborate, and more attentive to differences that emerge within this tradition in his *Sources of the Self* (Cambridge: Harvard University Press, 1989) (where he recognizes the difference between modernist and romantic versions of expression that I will soon take up, but he loses a little of his precision and his intensity because he belabors his differences with the continuing effects of the empiricist tradition, and because he provides readings of literary works that are not up to level of his philosophical intelligence. For Deleuze see his *Expressionism in Philosophy: Spinoza,* translated by Martin Joughim (New York: Zone Books, 1990). And for Frye, see the first chapter of his *Study of English Romanticism* (New York: Vintage, 1969), a work that does not refer directly to expressivism but relocates the coordinates of Christian culture in accord with a primary focus on subjective agency. I should add that Deleuze's critiques of Enlightenment versions of the subject would get us closer to the critical force of the Yeats poems I will study, but at the cost of losing their involvement within the romantic tradition that Taylor describes superbly. I do base my discussion of expression on Deleuze in my *Expressivist Agency and Expressivist Ethics* (Oxford: Blackwells, 1994), where I also substantiate some of the criticisms of Taylor and of poststructural theory that I will make all too briefly below.

5. I quote from Nancy's "Introduction" to *Who Comes After the Subject,* ed. by Nancy, Eduardo Cadava, and Peter Connor (Princeton: Princeton University Press, 1991), 6.

6. *Poems of W.B. Yeats,* 345–46.

7. Wallace Stevens, *The Collected Poems of Wallace Stevens* (New York: Alfred Knopf, 1954), 534.

Works Cited

Altieri, Charles. *Expressivist Agency and Expressivist Ethics,* Oxford: Blackwells, 1994.

Deleuze, Gilles. *Expressionism in Philosophy: Spinoza.* Translated by Martin Joughim. New York: Zone Books, 1990.

Frye, Northrop. *Study of English Romanticism.* New York: Vintage, 1969.

Nancy, Jean-Luc. "Introduction." *Who Comes After the Subject,* edited by Nancy, Eduardo Cadava, and Peter Connor. Princeton: Princeton University Press, 1991.

Rajchman, John. *Philosophical Events.* New York: Columbia University Press, 1991.

Stevens, Wallace. *The Collected Poems of Wallace Stevens.* New York: Alfred Knopf, 1954.

Taylor, Charles. *Hegel.* Cambridge: Cambridge University Press, 1985.

———. *Sources of the Self.* Cambridge: Harvard University Press, 1989.

Yeats, William Butler. *The Poems of W.B. Yeats.* Edited by Richard J. Finneran. New York: Macmillan, 1983.

Epistemological Empathy:
A. R. Ammons and Jorie Graham

Perception of an object costs
Precise the Object's loss—
Perception in itself a Gain
Replying to its Price—

The Object Absolute—is nought—
Perception sets it fair
And then upbraids a Perfectness
That situates so far—
　　　　　　　　　　—Emily Dickinson

EMILY DICKINSON'S PHILOSOPHICALLY CRYPTIC POEM MANIFESTS THE
basic transcendental view of the poet's epistemological approach
to her object. The object is what it is through the very perception
of the poet. The object is constituted by the perceiving human
subject. By means of language, and by his/her particular use of
language, the poet creates, or rather evokes and constitutes, the
world as s/he sees it. The first two lines of Dickinson's poem
indicate that the world, the objects that are being perceived, are
not the things in themselves. This goes along with the Kantian
argument that the thing in itself can never be known. The thing
we know is always the result, or rather a combination of, the
empirical presence of the object and the a priori forms of cognition and perception of the human being. This epistemological
view originated in the Cartesian "first principle" of the *cogito
ergo sum*. After Descartes had literally annihilated the objective
world by his method of doubting, he found himself isolated in
a universe in which he could only be certain of his own existence as a result of his being conscious of something (*cogito*).
Descartes's reintroduction of the lost world by way of his arguments for the existence of God was a philosophical failure and

43

has remained one to this day. The world was left in suspense, dangling and waiting to be constituted by the human subject. Immanuel Kant's transcendental theory of the process of cognition stands in the line of this tradition, and so do Edmund Husserl's reflections on Descartes's principle in his *Cartesian Meditations.* No wonder, then, that the poet has been regarded as the "maker" of the world,[1] all the more so since the very words poet/poetry are derived from the Greek *poiesis,* meaning "to make." Even A. W. E. O'Shaughnessy's late-nineteenth-century poem bears witness to this Cartesian tradition by calling the poet a "music-maker, a dreamer of dreams, a world-loser and world-forsaker, a mover and shaker of the world."[2]

An escape from this epistemological trap has been offered by Existentialist philosophers in the twentieth century, such as for instance, by Martin Heidegger. He refuses to theoretically separate the human subject from his objective world and, instead, places him right into the world. Cognition then is no longer an act of constitution, which is also reflected in his theory of language.

In the following analysis, I will take a close look at two poems by the contemporary American poets A. R. Ammons and Jorie Graham. These poems offer a different epistemological approach in the form of empathy, although their empathetic procedures vary in perspective, degree, and consequence.[3]

A. R. Ammons's conceptions of the world are based on subtle philosophical, rather than scientific, ways of thinking. With few exceptions, Ammons's poems do not contain a human "you." In her review of Ammons's book *Briefings* (1970), Helen Vendler says: "The poetry [Ammons] is best able to write is deprived of almost everything other poets have used, notably *people* [italics added] and adjectives."[4]

Within the tradition of American poetry, especially nature poetry, Ammons is most closely related to Ralph Waldo Emerson in the nineteenth century;[5] as far as contemporary American poetry is concerned, he is most likely to be compared with Gary Snyder. In spite of the parallels, however, there are also differences between them.

Ammons shares with Emerson man's longing for unity and harmony with the universe, although for Ammons they always remain separate entities:

> Emerson and Ammons share a nature that on the level of experience or confrontation cannot be humanized. Yet they share also a Tran-

scendental belief that one can come to a unity, at least in the poor good of the theory. Their common tone is a curious chill, a tang of other-than-human relationship to an Oversoul or Overall that is not nature, yet breaks through into nature. Like Emerson, its founder, Ammons is a poet of the American Sublime, and a residue of this primordial strength abides in all of his work.[6]

Whereas Emerson's individual is self-reliant, Ammons's is "humble" and far from being anthropocentric: "Ammons's wish to think with the mind of the universe, to comprehend reality not simply with anthropocentric vanity but truly from within, to put the motion of mind among all other physical motions, to become not a single vector but the resultant of all vectors, is his most ambitious aim."[7] Language, too, plays a more subordinate role for Ammons than it does for Emerson. Language serves to make present that which is beyond words.[8]

Ammons shares with Gary Snyder his distinct ecological attitude. The latter, however, is much more vehement and explicit in his message, all the more so since he decidedly confesses to the "counter-culture," than Ammons whose ecological engagement is less obtrusive though not less insistent. Ammons also differs from Snyder's Imagist and Objectivist ways of writing in that his style is more philosophical and reflective. What the two of them particularly share, though, is their scientific perspective:

> While science is founded on the idea of order, and while that idea certainly exerts a hold on Ammons, he is simultaneously drawn to that which eludes order, to the unpredictable and changing. The respective manifestations of order and disorder, characteristically found together in his poetry, contend for his allegiance, and he makes some effort to synthesize the two. But this sensibility is such as to resist final resolutions.[9]

Nature poetry in the traditional sense describes, often in a very venerating, enthusiastic, romantic way, some concrete image of nature. The dialogue with nature, which Ammons prefers, plays a different role.[10]

Within contemporary American poetry, Ammons holds an exceptional position. As one of the greatest and most promising poets, he has been particularly hailed by the Yale-critic Harold Bloom.[11] Also, Helen Vendler has reserved for him a special place among the greatest of American contemporary poets.[12] Apart from Bloom and Vendler, however, Ammons has not been given the attention he deserves by American literary critics. Some of the criticism that has been published on Ammons's poetry has missed the depth of his poems, has only touched it on the surface. Ammons is often reproached for being too distant and inaccessible, not open to interpretation and evaluation. He is either misunderstood as a "philosophical poet"[13] who is too difficult in his message, or avoided as a "cold poet," an attribute that has even been accepted, to some extent, by Ammons himself.[14] But his poetry is especially characterized by his philosophical probing. It is this philosophical depth that makes his poetry special.

Ammons's closeness to Heidegger is obvious, both in regard to his ontological/metaphysical theory and his reflections on language. It does not seem to matter that, in an interview with myself, Ammons denied any influence of Heidegger's on his own thinking and writing.

According to Heidegger, the poet must place the things into the opening of truth in such a way that [the things] may reveal themselves in their Being, in their essence. The poet must not conceal the things through his words, but ought to prepare for their "arrival in the unconcealedness of truth":

> In the current view, language is held to be a kind of communication. It serves for verbal exchange and agreement, and in general for communicating. But language is not only and not primarily an audible and written expression of what is to be communicated. It not only puts forth in words and statements what is overtly or covertly intended to be communicated; language alone brings beings as beings into the open for the first time. Where there is no language, as in the being of stone, plant, and animal, there is also no openness of beings, and consequently no openness either of nonbeing and of the empty.[15]

This means that the poet must not interfere with the essence of things, but must try to convey their essence to the reader: "Sprache ist nicht primär Verständigungsmittel, sondern dem Menschen nicht eigenes aber übereignetes Mittel zur Eröffnung von Welt, d.h. von Seiendem. Diese Möglichkeit macht erst das Menschsein des Menschen aus" [Language is not primarily a means of communication, but a means of the human being to open up the world, that is to say beings. This possibility is what makes the human being a human being].[16] This opening up of the world, however, is not achieved by one individual human being, the individual does not remain in a solipsistic world: "Sprache gründet Welt. Welt ist Mitwelt. Sprache ist so primär Gespräch" [Language creates the world. World is a "being together." Therefore language is primarily conversation].[17] Ammons has postulated his ideas of the task of the poet in this Heideggerian sense in his poem "Poetics," whose title evokes the theme:

Poetics

I look for the way
things will turn
out spiralling from a center,
the shape
things will take to come forth in

so that the birch tree white
touched black at branches
will stand out
wind-glittering
totally its apparent self:

I look for the forms
things want to come as

from what black wells of possibility,
how a thing will
unfold:

not the shape on paper—though
that, too—but the
uninterfering means on paper:

not so much looking for the shape
as being available
to any shape that may be
summoning itself
through me

from the self not mine but ours.[18]

Ammons never places the human ego in the center of his poems; rather, he tries to free himself from an egocentric and anthropocentric view of the world. Nor does he attribute to the poet a superior position. Rather, he sees the poet as the mediator of truth in the above described sense. This becomes clear in the poem. The poet is a seeker rather than a knower and disposer: "The search is for a poetic incarnation, but it is also an abandonment of the search, a hope of poetic disincarnation, a way of overcoming by literally *undergoing* the separate self."[19] This search is to be understood in the sense of approaching things, their essence ("I look for"). The poet does not, as might be expected, look for the adequate means to describe things. Rather, he gropes his way to their proximity in order to tempt them out of their innermost Being so that they may show themselves in their essence: he looks for their form and shape. Ammons grants the things their independence. He does not dispose of them. This is explicitly expressed by the word "uninterfering" in the poem. Thus, it is the things themselves that spiral out of their center in order to become visible, it is the things themselves that take shape (first stanza). The theory of the first stanza is made concrete in the example of the second stanza: the birch tree presents and reveals its self ("totally its apparent self"). This line is bursting with meaning. The thing (in this case the birch tree) shows ("apparent") its self, its essence ("its . . . self," not itself) "totally." That is, the thing is not being presented by the poet as seen by him; rather, the thing shows itself, freely and completely. The contrast between black and white intensifies the analogy to Heidegger's notion of the thing's arrival in the unconcealedness of truth.[20] The following two lines, the third stanza so to speak, do not only continue the train of thought but they reflect the idea of the poem in their aesthetic beauty and perfection. These are achieved through the inversion of the sentence, the "as" being postponed to the end, which again places the poet's will, if not beneath so, on the same level with the will of the thing.

What is remarkable also is that the poet does not take for granted that there is only *one* form in which things can show themselves. The poet grants them a *choice* of several possible forms ("black wells of possibility"). He does not arrogate to know all those forms or their origin. The word "black" in this connection may be interpreted in the sense of "unknown" and "unavailable" to the poet. It is the poet's endeavor to find out how a thing opens itself, shows itself to him ("how a thing will unfold"). Thus remarks Helen R. Elam on this aspect: "There can be no utterance of permanence in Ammons' universe, only of things that speak and disappear, and this means that the poet has to be open to what the moment makes available to him, for each moment is

a potential threshold into the privileged continuum."[21] When
the thing then shows itself, the question arises for the poet as
to how he may write down that which has shown itself to him,
how "the thing in itself" may take shape on paper without the
poet himself interfering (*"uninterfering* means on paper").
Thus, he finally withdraws completely, leaves interference behind and is only a "means" that is available to the form ("being
available") in the sense that through him the things find their
own forms. Only thus does the poet succeed in approaching the
thing as well as in achieving unison with it: "the self not mine
but ours."

Yet this is a unity in which both the I and the thing remain
an entity of their own. For this unity is not to be understood in
the sense of a mystical fusion of man and nature. Rather, it is a
total empathy with either of them remaining a separate entity.
This empathy, this approaching of the other, between man and
nature, without interference with or disposal of the other, is
realized by Ammons very often by means of the dialogue. The
dialogue between man and nature thus becomes an unmistak-
able ecological message,[22] as nature becomes a partner to the
human being who has an ecological attitude.[23] Ammons's ecological attitude is a holistic one, he rejects a cutting up of reality
and pleads, like Friedrich von Weizsäcker, for leaving reality as
a whole.[24]

Empathy characterizes man's relationship to nature in Ammons's poems. Man is open to nature, waiting in order to be able
to hear and see nature. "The position of the self, like the poem's
is one of great risk but also of informed openness, a readiness to
strike up conversations anywhere and map out new excursions
everywhere."[25] This openness is therefore characterized by a
lack of intentionality. Ammons grants nature the possibility to
speak for herself. Although her language is borrowed, so to
speak, from the poet, nature still speaks for herself and is not
spoken about.

I think it is justified to call Ammons a philosophical poet, as
Hyatt Waggoner does: "I would like to call [Ammons] a philosophical poet—except that description might turn away some of
those who should read him, and except also that the phrase is
in part intrinsically misleading in its suggestion that he deals
principally in abstractions."[26] The poem "Poetics" offers his self-
definition as a poet who regards himself no longer as a maker,
not even as a seer in the Emersonian sense of the word, but

rather as a "perceiver" who leaves his self behind in order to feel himself into the thing in itself.

Empathy is also the keyword to Jorie Graham's epistemological approach to her object. In her poem "San Sepolcro," the object is not part of nature but a man-made painting. The poet's intention towards this painting is not only to perceive it but to understand it. Knowing and understanding respectively in Ammons's and in Graham's poems imply subtle differences in meaning. Whereas Ammons's "Poetics" suggests a principal mode of cognition of the thing other than himself, Graham's poem reveals a hermeneutic perspective that means to transcend the boundaries between the human subject and the object to be "understood." The key line "come, we can go in," which keeps recurring in modifications throughout the whole poem, represents a revolutionary approach to the object in that her empathy moves also beyond the boundaries of time and space.

San Sepolcro

In this blue light
　　I can take you there,
snow having made me
　　a world of bone
seen through to. This
　　is my house,

my section of Etruscan
　　wall, my neighbor's
lemontrees, and, just below
　　the lower church,
the airplane factory.
　　A rooster

crows all day from mist
　　outside the walls.
There's milk on the air,
　　ice on the oily
lemonskins. How clean
　　the mind is,

holy grave. It is this girl
　　by Piero
della Francesca, unbuttoning
　　her blue dress,

her mantle of weather,
   to go into

labor. Come, we can go in.
   It is before
the birth of god. No-one
   has risen yet
to the museums, to the assembly
   line—bodies

and wings—to the open air
   market. This is
what the living do: go in.
   It's a long way.
And the dress keeps opening
   from eternity

to privacy, quickening.
   Inside, at the heart,
is tragedy, the present moment
   forever stillborn,
but going in, each breath
   is a button

coming undone, something terribly
   nimble-fingered
finding all of the stops.[27]

Jorie Graham grew up in Italy and then moved to the United States. She received a number of grants and awards and has published four books of poetry. *Erosion* came out in 1983. Her European background is reflected again and again in references to cultural documents, particularly paintings.

In "San Sepolcro" she describes the famous painting by Piero della Francesca, his "Madonna del Parto." As one can read in art books on Piero della Francesca, "the iconography of Piero's pregnant Madonna seems to be unique in Italian art."[28] It may be helpful to know that this particular painting is not to be found in a museum (despite the concrete mentioning of museums in the poem), but in a chapel in the small village of Monterchio. Near Borgo San Sepolcro lies Monterchio:

a small village, and there, in the chapel of the cemetery, is a fresco which, after passing for generations unnoticed, was identified in 1889 . . . as an undoubted work of Piero della Francesca. . . . The subject of the fresco is the standing figure of the Virgin of the size of life. Two angels, standing one on either side of her, hold back falling curtains of rich material, and thus seem to exhibit the Virgin to the worshippers in the chapel. The face is sad and wistful. . . . The impression of languor and sorrow which the first glance at the figure produces, arises naturally from the signs of impending maternity which are rendered with verisimilitude sufficient to have won for the Virgin, in the mouths of the adjacent countrywomen, the name of 'Madonna del Parto'.[29]

Contemplation, abstraction, and realism are trademarks of Piero's art and characterize this painting as well. Another important aspect is his combination of the sublime and the common. In this painting, for example, the angels resemble ordinary women, in spite of their wings.[30]

It is not of little importance that the lyrical I describes her approach to the painting as a literal way, through the Italian landscape, through the cemetery, into the chapel, and right *into* the painting. The lyrical I also seems to adopt the role of a guide, presenting herself as a means (compare to Ammons), an uninterfering means of vision and understanding. The poet carefully opens up one perspective after another in order to safely guide her reader to the final stop. This is not only indicated by the word "stops" at the very end of the poem but also by the fact that the last stanza consists of only three lines as opposed to all the other six-line stanzas. The poem therefore ends in the very middle of the stanza, signaling that we have arrived at the center, that we have penetrated the object.

Perspective and space are Graham's main poetic means to proceed on her "guided tour." Her opening up of perspectives and the gradual penetration to the center, the core of the painting, resemble the idea of the "Chinese boxes." The procedure is from light and air to the Italian landscape to the church to the grave to the painting. She does not even stop there. Rather, she invites the reader to step into the painting, to step beyond space and to step backwards in time, to step—by means of imagination—into the situation displayed, into the woman's fears, into her blue dress, into the actual happening: of giving birth, of being born. The lyrical I has indeed assumed the role of the guide. This I, however, has transcended the boundaries of her physical body, she represents something more essential, more knowing, unlimited, yet all the more tangible. This is expressed right in the first stanza where the "blue light" provides the atmosphere of transcendence, and she herself is a "world of bone, [white bone], seen through to." (The term "lyrical I" here refers both to the biographical I of the poet and to a potential I with which the reader may identify). The bone imagery, of course, links up immediately with the cemetery and the "holy grave." This I is therefore one beyond death and life, presenting both death and life. This expansion, or dissolution, of the lyrical I provides a perspective that covers historical and temporal distances. The moment in time depicted by the painting is that before the birth of God. Only in historical retrospect, which encompasses the knowledge that has spread between the then and the now, can that knowledge (of the birth as well as of the death of God) convey meaning on the contents of the painting. In order to emphasize both her awareness of the present moment in time and the necessity of bridging the temporal and spatial gap between the present and the past depicted in the painting, Graham clearly differentiates between an outside and an inside perspective. It is not only her description of nature ("lemontrees," "rooster") that creates an outside realistic world; also her mentioning of the church and the airplane factory contributes to a realistic setting, particularly since the latter also fixes this outside perspective to the present, the twentieth century. The "walls" in the second stanza are an adequate metaphor to mark the gap between the outside and the inside. The inside perspective is that of the mind. It is certainly no coincidence that the mind is, though ambivalently, equated with the "holy grave": "How clean / the mind is, / holy grave." The enjambment provides for the possibility of reading the holy grave as an apposition to the mind, yet at the same time, because of the splitting of the line into two separate stanzas, also indicates a crucial difference. The holy grave evokes associations both with death and resurrection. It is the mind that buries/preserves and also creates/resurrects. The play between the two perspectives is continued after she has entered the inside, the mind.

In the second part of the poem, Jorie Graham juxtaposes the museum and the contents of the painting. She thereby manages to counterbalance the present, the contemporary spectator, and the meaning of the painting, which has to be grasped behind the walls of time and space. On the one hand, she is talking about the painting by Piero della Francesca that is being looked at by museum visitors of today, thus emphasizing the gap between the perceiving subject and the object; on the other, she approaches the time-and-space scope of the painting itself, which has to be approached by means of one's imagination, in one's own mind. The spectator who follows the guiding lyrical I therefore does not stop in front of the painting but rather steps into it. The poet manages perfectly to bridge the gap between the outside and the inside in the transition from the fourth to the fifth stanza: "to go into / labor. Come, we can go in." Not only does the enjambment visually present and bridge the gap, but the verbal parallelism ("to go in"), too, allows the reader to feel and think himself into the woman, the situation, the painting. The statement "it is before the birth of god" cannot really be grasped by the reader in its full meaning, as the reader's knowledge of the birth and death of God interferes with his/her capacity to feel himself/herself into the historical situation. The concept of God becomes alive in the human mind after he has been born. Once we have stopped inside (the painting), we ourselves experience the tragedy of the situation. It is exactly at this moment that the painting becomes alive. The moment caught in the painting is "forever stillborn." But imagination gives life to this stillborn moment, because our minds comprise the past and the present. Thus, we can both step backwards in time and re-animate the past moment by means of our memory and knowledge. But the moment does not become alive through the perception of the human being. It becomes alive as the human being participates in the moment. And yet this going into the moment of birth by a mind that transcends space and time is being stopped, stopped by the nimble fingers that unbutton the dress, "This is what the living do: go in." This ambiguous and yet revealing line suggests the never-ending process of going in. The transition from the fourth to the fifth stanza, having the word "labor" in the middle, also indicates that "going in" is painful. The human mind, in this poem, is the key to the various ways of "going in," the human mind, which Graham calls the "holy grave" (this is also indicated in the title of the poem). This comparison not only comprises life and death, resurrection and immortality; it also conjures up the potential of the human archetypal memory. Come, we can go in—is an encouraging invitation to the readers to feel their way into that which is to be understood. The anthropocentric superiority of man in the traditional subject-object relation no longer prevails. The mind is not constituting but expanding, fusing empathetically with its object without abandoning its being in a particular historical point in time.

In their poems, Ammons and Graham have demonstrated that the separating line between subject and object can, indeed, be overstepped. And perception need not necessarily cost the object's loss. Rather, going in is an alternative way toward gaining the object.

Notes

1. Cf. my interpretation of Emily Dickinson in Gudrun M. Grabher, *Emily Dickinson: Das transzendentale Ich* (Heidelberg: Carl Winter Universitätsverlag, 1981).

2. In Elizabeth Drew, *Poetry. A Modern Guide to Its Understanding and Enjoyment* (New York: Dell Publishing, 1959), 16.

3. I have dealt with these two poems in regard to the question of the "lyrical You" in the following publications: Gudrun M. Grabher, *Das lyrische Dy: Du-Vergessenheit und Möglichkeiten der Du-Bestimmung in der amerikanischen Dichtung* (Heidelberg: Carl Winter Universitätsverlag, 1989) and Gudrun M. Grabher, "The Female Vision in the American Poetry of the 1980s," in *Women in Search of Literary Space*, ed. Gudrun M. Grabher and Maureen Devine (Tübingen: Gunter Narr, 1991), 68–84.

4. Helen Vendler, "New Books in Review: Ammons, Berryman, Cummings," *The Yale Review*, 62, no. 3 (1973), 419.

5. Ammons's relatedness to Emerson has especially been emphasized by Harold Bloom. When asked in an interview with Cynthia Haythe whether Ammons felt too much compared with Emerson by his reviewers, he answered: "I don't think so. I really didn't read Emerson that much or that well before Harold Bloom started speaking of him. When Harold began to speak of my connection to Emerson, I went back myself to try and confirm or renounce this thing, and I found, in nearly every paragraph, a man speaking my central concerns more beautifully than I could speak them myself, there's just no doubt about it. I would *love* to renounce it because no one wishes to be that much like or influenced by anyone. But Emerson says the very thoughts that I think I've come up with on my own. I certainly haven't paid much attention to him, but I can open his work at almost any place and see a better thinker and a better writer saying my material for me, for the most part. "An Interview with A. R. Ammons," *Contemporary Literature* 21, no. 2 (1980), 186ff.

6. Harold Bloom, "The New Transcendentalism: The Visionary Strain in Merwin, Ashbery, and Ammons," *The Chicago Review* 24, no. 3 (1973), 42.

7. Helen Vendler, *The Music of What Happens. Poems, Poets, Critics* (Cambridge, Mass.: Harvard University Press, 1988), 319.

8. Cf. D. I. Grossvogel, "Interview. / A. R. Ammons." *Diacritics* 3, no. 4 (1973), 47. In this interview Ammons remarks on language: ". . . Laotse says that nothing that can be said in words is worth saying. He means, I think, that by the time we have embodied into limitation any sort of reality, it has limited itself out of the total adumbration." 47. Cf. also Wilson O. Clough, *The Necessary Earth. Nature and Solitude in American Literature* (Austin: University of Texas Press, 1964), 80. In his poem "Motion" Ammons also deals with language in this sense.

9. Alan Holder, *A. R. Ammons* (Boston: Twayne Publishers, 1978), 17.

10. Cf. Grabher, *Das lyrische Du.*

11. In various of his works Bloom praises Ammons in superlatives.

12. Cf. Vendler, *The Music of What Happens.*

13. "I would like to call him a *philosophical poet* [italics added]—except that description might turn away some of those who should read him, and except also that the phrase is in part intrinsically misleading in its suggestion that he deals principally in abstractions." Hyatt Waggoner, "The Poetry of A. R. Ammons: Some Notes and Reflections," *Salmagundi* 22–23 (1973), 287. "Not the least of A. R. Ammons' virtues is that he is an original *philosopher* [italics added] in his poetry, though often he parades in the guise of philosopher-as-anti-poet." Lawrence Lieberman, *Unassigned Frequencies. American Poetry in Review, 1964–1977* (Urbana: University of Illinois Press, 1977), 62.

14. In an interview, Cynthia Haythe asked Ammons, "How would you reply to those reviewers who accuse you of being a cold poet," to which Ammons responded: "I would say they're right. There is an aspect of my work that's defensive. I should appear cold to almost anyone on first contact with my work. But it seems to me that the more of my work they know, the more it returns to them, the more another nature—welcoming and generous, I think—would begin to emerge. Because I don't offer myself quickly or easily to anyone. I'm very defensive and withdrawn." "An Interview with A. R. Ammons," *Contemporary Literature* 21, no. 2 (1980), 186ff.

15. Martin Heidegger, *The Origin of the Work of Art,* in Martin Heidegger, *Basic Writings,* ed. David Farrell Krell (New York: Harper & Row, 1977), 185.

16. Irmgard Bock, *Heideggers Sprachdenken* (Meisenheim am Glan: Verlag AntonHain, 1966), 54. Translation mine.

17. Ibid., 55. Translation mine.

18. A. R. Ammons, *Briefings. Poems Small and Easy* (New York: W. W. Norton, 1971), 44ff.

19. Richard Howard, "The Spent Seer Consigns Order to the Vehicle of Change," in *A. R. Ammons,* ed. Harold Bloom (New York: Chelsea House Publishers, 1986), 53.

20. Hyatt Waggoner (in regard to "Poetics") has also referred to the parallels with Heidegger: "In the inseparable union of physics and metaphysics in Ammons' imagination, the emphasis may have shifted a little from the *meta* to the *physics,* but the union has not been dissolved, as of course it must not be if poetry is to continue to have noetic value (Heidegger's 'What Are Poets For?' in his recent *Poetry, Language, Thought* is relevant here. . . .)." "Notes and Reflections," in *A. R. Ammons,* 68.

21. Helen Regueiro Elam, "Radiances and Dark Consolations," in *A. R. Ammons,* 268.

22. "A strain in Ammons [is] ecological . . . ." Harold Bloom, *The Ringers in the Tower. Studies in Romantic Tradition* (Chicago: The University of Chicago Press, 1971), 270. In *Tape for the Turn of the Year* (New York: W. W. Norton, 1972) Ammons says:

> ecology is my word: tag
> me with that: come
> there:
> you will find yourself
> in a firmless country:
> centers & peripheries
> in motion,
> organic,
> interrelations!

(p. 112)

23. Cf. Hans Sachsse, *Ökologische Philosophie. Natur—Technik—Gesellschaft* (Darmstadt: Wissenschaftliche Buchgesellschaft, 1984).

24. Karl Heinz Kreeb, *Ökologie und menschliche Umwelt. Geschichte—Bedeutung—Zukunftsaspekte I* (Stuttgart: Gustav Fischer Verlag, 1979), 171ff.

25. John E. Sitter, "About Ammons' *Sphere*," *The Massachusetts Review* 19, no. 1 (1978), 212.

26. Hyatt H. Waggoner, "The Poetry of A. R. Ammons: Some Notes and Reflections," *Salmagundi* 22–23 (1973), 287.

27. Jorie Graham, "San Sepolcro," in *Erosion* (Princeton: Princeton University Press, 1983), 2ff.

28. Kenneth Clark, *Piero della Francesca*, Complete Edition (London: Phaidon, 1969, 2d edition), 226.

29. W. G. Waters, *Piero della Francesca* (London: George Bell and Sons, 1901), 56ff.

30. Cf. Albert Skira, *Der Geschmack unserer Zeit. Piero della Francesca* (Genf: Editions d'Art Albert Skira, 1954) and Herbert Alexander Stützer, *Die Italienische Renaissance* (Köln: DuMont Buchverlag, 1977).

Works Cited

Ammons, A. R. *Briefings. Poems Small and Easy.* New York: W. W. Norton, 1971.

———. *Tape for the Turn of the Year.* New York: W. W. Norton, 1972.

Bloom, Harold. "The New Transcendentalism: The Visionary Strain in Merwin, Ashbery, and Ammons," *The Chicago Review* 24, no. 3 (1973): 25–43.

———. *The Ringers in the Tower. Studies in Romantic Tradition.* Chicago and London: The University of Chicago Press, 1971.

Bock, Irmgard. *Heideggers Sprachdenken.* Meisenheim am Glan: Verlag Anton Hain, 1966.

Clark, Kenneth. *Piero della Francesca.* Complete Edition. London & New York: Phaidon, 1969.

Clough, Wilson O. *The Necessary Earth. Nature and Solitude in American Literature.* Austin: University of Texas Press, 1964.

Drew, Elizabeth. *Poetry. A Modern Guide to Its Understanding and Enjoyment.* New York: Dell Publishing, 1959.

Elam, Helen Regueiro. "Radiances and Dark Consolations," in *A. R. Ammons.* ed. Harold Bloom. New York, New Haven, Philadelphia: Chelsea House Publishers, 1986, 263–85.

Grabher, Gudrun. *Emily Dickinson: Das transzendentale Ich.* Heidelberg: Carl Winter Universitätsverlag, 1981.

Grabher, Gudrun M. *Das lyrische Du: Du-Vergessenheit und Möglichkeiten der Du-Bestimmung in der amerikanischen Dichtung.* Heidelberg: Carl Winter Universitätsverlag, 1989.

———. "The Female Vision in the American Poetry of the 1980s." In *Women in Search of Literary Space,* eds. Gudrun M. Grabher and Maureen Devine. Tübingen: Gunter Narr, 1991, 68–84.

Graham, Jorie. *Erosion.* Princeton: Princeton University Press, 1983.

Grossvogel, D. I. "Interview / A. R. Ammons." *Diacritics* 3, 4 (1973): 47–53.

Haythe, Cynthia. "An Interview with A. R. Ammons." *Contemporary Literature* 21, 2 (1980): 173–90.

Heidegger, Martin. *The Origin of the Work of Art.* In *Martin Heidegger. Basic Writings,* ed. David Farrell Krell. New York: Harper & Row, 1977, 143–87.

Holder, Alan. *A. R. Ammons.* Boston: Twayne Publishers, 1978.

Howard, Richard. "The Spent Seer Consigns Order to the Vehicle of Change," *A. R. Ammons,* ed. Harold Bloom. New York, New Haven, Philadelphia: Chelsea House Publishers, 1986, 33–56.

Johnson, Thomas H. *The Poems of Emily Dickinson,* vol. 2. Cambridge: The Belknap Press of Harvard University Press, 1968.

Kreeb, Karl Heinz. *Ökologie und menschliche Umwelt. Geschichte—Bedeutung—Zukunftsaspekte.* Stuttgart: New York: Gustav Fischer Verlag, 1979.

Lieberman, Lawrence. *Unassigned Frequencies. American Poetry in Review, 1964–1977.* Urbana, Chicago, London: University of Illinois Press, 1977.

Sachsse, Hans. *Ökologische Philosophie. Natur—Technik—Gesellschaft.* Darmstadt: Wissenschaftliche Buchgesellschaft, 1984.

Sitter, John E. "About Ammons' *Sphere,*" *The Massachusetts Review* 19, 1 (1978): 201–12.

Skira, Albert. *Der Geschmack unserer Zeit. Piero della Francesca.* Genf: Editions d'Art Albert Skira, 1954.

Stützer, Herbert Alexander. *Die Italienische Renaissance.* Köln: DuMont Buchverlag, 1977.

Vendler, Helen. "New Books in Review: Ammons, Berryman, Cummings," *The Yale Review* 62, no. 3 (1973): 412–25.

Vendler, Helen. *The Music of What Happens. Poems, Poets, Critics.* Cambridge, Mass.: Harvard University Press, 1988.

Waggoner, Hyatt H. "The Poetry of A. R. Ammons: Some Notes and Reflections," *Salmagundi* 22–23 (1973): 285–93.

Waggoner, Hyatt H. "Notes and Reflections." in *A. R. Ammons.* ed. Harold Bloom. New York, New Haven, Philadelphia: Chelsea House Publishers, 1986, 63–71.

Waters, W. G. *Piero della Francesca.* London: George Bell and Sons, 1901.

Lyrical Variation of Tone in Stevens's Poetry

ALAIN SUBERCHICOT

Aɴʏ ᴇxᴘᴇʀɪᴇɴᴄᴇ ᴏғ ʀᴇᴀᴅɪɴɢ Sᴛᴇᴠᴇɴs ʀᴇᴠᴇᴀʟs ᴇxᴛʀᴇᴍᴇ ᴠᴀʀɪᴀʙɪʟ-ity of tone. Tonal difference is one basic aspect of the texture of his verse. Stevens can be amusing, even clownish, and develop a sense of the tragedy of the human predicament, so that one wonders whether contradiction may not have been run through the verse. The tonal variation is so radical that the poet does not seem to be in control of the tonal effects produced by his lines. At times, the poetry loses much of its habitual capacity to convey emotions. It sounds like mere word-play or betrays intellectual detachment. Deliberate anticlimax in the way of gay or serious irony is not infrequent. The usual criticism leveled at Stevens by those of his opponents who feel that his aestheticism is an instance of poetic misconduct is, however, mitigated by the tonal difference at work in many of his poems. It is my contention that Stevens's variability of tone is, to him, highly protective insofar as the aestheticism most often invoked in the receptions of Stevens's work demands of the poet to constantly expand the scope of lyrical expression. By fiddling with intellectual detach-ment and diffidence, and by moving swiftly from a tone of banter to a tone of pathos, and on to narratives of social comedy, Stevens couples the daimonic with the clownish. He thus celebrates a sense of community and an epistemology that one should under-stand as a celebration of shared experience. He also controls what he felt might be one pitfall of beauty, the danger that too much beauty might isolate him from the common run of humanity.

While it is probably true that Stevens never worried much about being popular as a poet, we find no evidence of an unwill-ingness to share meaning and to offer his poems as a test of personal strength for other poets and readers to assess their personal and aesthetic force. Tonal variation thus serves as an encomium of shared subjectivity, which is Stevens's best resistance to interpretations of his poetry that tend to entrap his work within the confines of an egotistic and indifferent aestheticism. My analysis of Stevens's poetry comes as a continuation of what seems to me to have been the major debate in Stevens criticism over the past decades, one opposing Gerald Bruns,[1] who views Stevens as the aesthete without a moral purpose to his aestheticism, a poet without a regard for shared experience, and Charles Altieri, who extols lyricism in Stevens as "a way of realizing his own difference, his own claim to individual identity, then of positing that difference in such a way that it promises to yield to others a sense of similar orientations in their imaginative investments."[2]

I view tonal differences within Stevens's writing as the trick of the aesthete who uses them to make his verse into a moment of cultural celebration of the community. The conflict with meter that is at work in Stevens's poetry is not especially dire to him. He probably welcomed such a conflict as a chance to enroll in his verse the rhythms of a poetic tradition that preceded modernism and thus let him remain audible to the more formal trends of American poetry.

Voice Versus Meter

Where exactly does Stevens stand in the conflict of voice with writing? No doubt there are historical reasons within American poetry that made Stevens respond to this conflict long before Jacques Derrida developed his well-known critique of phonocentrism. Besides, I do not think that Derrida ever wanted to demonstrate that there is an opposition between voice and writing.[3] Stevens, the way I see it, felt that the living voice of the poet was given vitality by the haunting presence of rhythmical patterns reminiscent of those of nineteenth century British and American romanticism. In those rhythms, he felt that voice was at odds with social pressure, and that this seminal conflict enabled to celebrate both the poet's subjectivity and a sense of togetherness—a benign version of social pressure. The Emersonian heritage, which is now thought to be strong in Stevens, if we consider Richard Poirier's latest examination of this,[4] was no encouragement, we may surmise, for the poet to preserve his vocal identity in the face of social pressure inasmuch as, to Poirier, in the Emersonian tradition, it is the business of the poet to embody a total culture that is greater than the artist's. On the other hand, Harold Bloom, who is an idealist, demonstrates in *Figures of Capable Imagination* that Emerson, in "Self Reliance," evinces belief that preserving one's own voice will make any man scorn to imitate another. Stevens was probably hesitating as to the capacity of language to be endowed with the power to redeem man's fragility when confronting social and cultural values.

Conflicting with meter is the result of the poet's quest of the nonpoetic, namely an experience of community beyond language. It is true that conflicting with meter is also, as Timothy Steele has demonstrated in *Missing Measures; Modern Poetry and the Revolt Against Meter*, one standard attitude of most modern poets who feel that accents are artificial because they think that scansion has to be made audible, whereas English has a higher degree of naturalness than a mere succession of stressed and unstressed syllables.[5] Stevens is deeper than this, since he reacts with epistemological concerns in mind, thus overlooking the merely external question of sound patterns. Examining "Ideas of Order at Key West," one realizes that the female voice talking explores the chaos of the sea, rejecting her own attempts at ordering the universe of which it is a part:

> She sang beyond the genius of the sea.
> The water never formed to mind or voice,
> Like a body wholly body, fluttering
> Its empty sleeves; and yet its mimic motion
> Made constant cry, caused constantly a cry,
> That was not ours although we understood,
> Inhuman, of the veritable ocean.[6]

These unrhymed iambic pentameters produce an impression of artificial superimposition, thus also mimicking the artificial attempt at ordering, of the woman's voice trying to woo the sea into a regular rhythm that would contradict its true nature. Is the nonpoetic here grasped? It is, but in a negative sort of way proceeding from the resistance of the sea to the order of the mind. Prevailing over difference among tones is the difference within tone. Instances such as this one are common: "Made constant cry, caused constantly a cry" is a fascinating example of writing from within the conflict of voice and meter, because the line reads as an iambic pentameter of the most regular sort, and also reads as two parallel statements juxtaposing two opposing rhythmical units at odds with each other yet in close conjunc-

tion. The very title of the poem is oxymoronic in essence: can
one think of a more unsuitable place than Key West for an idea
of order to emerge? Stevens does not seem to care for an answer.
Confronting the nonpoetic, facing the sea which is viewed as the
locus for the senses to test their powers, the female speaker feels
the world is resisting her, causing the universe that the senses
reveal to accept submission after a while. We realize that such
submission is illusory, though, it is conveyed to us with a calm
assurance that sounds misleading. Indeed, Stevens wanted it to
appear as such:

> And when she sang, the sea,
> Whatever self it had, became the self
> That was her song, for she was the maker. (*CP* 129)

This instance of transubstantiation is hard to believe, and reveals its uncertain status, close on mock metamorphosis, because it remains largely an operation of the mind that feeds
on the need to compensate for the failing hortative powers of
language. The tonal variations one finds in these lines are largely
the record of the failure to persuade. Tonal variation is thus a
matter of posture when facing an alien world one does not approach with sufficient flexibility.

How far is the female voice, whose lyrical inflections reveal
emotional involvement, a public voice? The voice at war with
meter is the voice of shared experience. From a thematic view-
point, the refusal of the world to conform to our whims is one
aspect of the human predicament that will make Stevens's poetry most familiar to many. Moreover, one voice that does not
conform to meter will also be one recognition of the validity of
resistance as an awareness-building experience that reinforces
the self. A strong self is the best appeal for readers to construct
empathy with the text. Moreover, Harold Bloom eulogized the
aesthetic resilience of Stevens, thereby suggesting that the years
of *Ideas of Order* were quite productive, when he expressed the
view, in *Wallace Stevens; the Poems of Our Climate*, that the
poet "rarely made the error of reducing any of his own poems
to ideas of order alone."[7] Helen Vendler in turn was impressed
by the "discontinuity between two orders, the voice of nature
and the voice of the singer." However, she considered that such
discrepancy "does not in itself establish any difference in magnitude between the two orders."[8] Does one find at all, as Helen
Vendler thinks we do, an order in the voice of nature and an-

other, of a more cultural sort, in the female voice? This would be a fine opportunity to track down tonal variations and these voices would then depend their existence upon an epistemological gap of the most fascinating sort. The final stanza in the poem belies, it seems to me, this insight. The "blessed rage for order" is entirely the maker's:

> Oh! Blessed rage for order, pale Ramon,
> The maker's rage to order words of the sea,
> Words of the fragrant portals, dimly-starred,
> And of ourselves and of our origins,
> In ghostlier demarcations, keener sounds.
>
> (*CP* 130)

Helen Vendler adopts the perspective of a successful ordering of nature by the maker's voice, thus choosing the stance of a pragmatist who disregards, unlike Richard Poirier,[9] the negative consequences of pragmatism, when the speech act fails to shape or organize what comes within its range. The work of Stevens is entirely the work of someone expressing doubt as to the capacity of language to signify exactly what the author intends. The ironical tones that one finds in the address to Ramon Fernandez, the fictional hero, signal that the poet wishes to control the impulse to believe in the transfiguration of the universe through the mere action of such poor devices as fumbling words enraged at the idea of controlling something beyond control.

Stevens's poetic or even linguistic skepticism is too strong to permit a stabilized tone. The smooth lyricism of the romantic confessional poem is an impossibility that Stevens considers half-wistfully and half-playfully. "Sailing after lunch" hardly has any of the wealth of imaginative investment of "Ideas of Order at Key West," where poetic skepticism still allowed a glimmer of hope to filter through. "Sailing after lunch" revels in unbelief, but the conflict with meter is still there:

> Mon Dieu, hear the poet's prayer.
> The romantic should be here.
> The romantic should be there.
> It ought to be everywhere.
> But the romantic must remain,
>
> . . . .
>
> Mon Dieu, and must never again return.
>
> (*CP* 120)

Is Stevens praying at all? The use of a French word is here, as usual, the sign of word-play, which shows intellectual detachment and reveals a high degree of emotional control. The parallels that Stevens's intellectual detachment produces shatter any attempt at the rhythmical reading that would sound meter without any artificial emphasis. If we were to scan, we would produce more of a metronomic than a musical effect, so that it is the tone of comedy that comes naturally to us whenever we read this poem aloud, a tone that does not carry to our ears the organization of the lines into metrical feet.

Preserving Lyricism

The freedom with which Stevens adopts the tone of comedy in his verse raises the issue of the status of lyricism. Does the tone of comedy belong with the category of lyrical verse, or does Stevens embrace in so doing another sub-genre, the absurdist piece? "Sailing after lunch" is a challenge to the critic because one hesitates to classify it as lyrical verse. Romanticism seems to be dead and gone, and one is here at a loss to see lyricism as a valid purpose that the poet can make his own. It is true that speaking of the tone of a piece implies examining both its musical quality and its manner of expression. The musical quality of a piece can be aggressively antilyrical yet refrain from challenging its modernism. What is at stake is the possibility for a poem to oppose through its tonal variation the metaphysical perspective which it is the constant temptation of the lyrical poem to promote, what Emerson once tentatively called "the universal impulse to believe." Such belief, Emerson thought, proceeded from what he described as "the leading of the sentiment."[10] One feels, though, that Stevens is capable of preserving lyricism while negating the metaphysical foundations of poetry. To achieve this, Stevens must overcome metaphysics. What he does is that he preserves the rites of language, and tonal degradation of the emotional into the ludicrous or the merely playful is how he does it, while the critique of metaphysics is fully carried out. A short lyric, "Sad strains of a gay waltz," expresses Stevens's doubts on the question of aesthetic hope:

> The truth is that there comes a time
> When we can mourn no more over music
> That is so much motionless sound.

> (CP 121)

The critique of musicality, which would not concern someone like Stevens if we took this discussion of music at face value, is everywhere. What Stevens aims for here is the *universal impulse to believe*, as Emerson's words go. The title of the poem suggests that the waltz is gay because it celebrates intellectual power, that we may take to be the key to unbelief, yet the waltz remains one with sad strains because the undoing of metaphysics that it effects breeds the tonal manner of the somber lyric. In Stevens tonal variation is thus the result of the revision of romanticism at work all through his poetry, as Elizabeth A. Frost suggested in an article, with special emphasis on "Notes towards a Supreme Fiction."[11] Stevens expresses this adequately in the concluding lines of his gay waltz:

> Too many waltzes—The epic of disbelief
> Blares oftener and soon, will soon be constant.
> Some harmonious skeptic soon in a skeptical music
> Will unite these figures of men and their shapes
> Will glisten again with motion, the music
> Will be motion and full of shadows.
>
> (*CP* 122)

It is upon the fragments of the romantic lyric that a new variety of expression is built up. There is an epic dimension attached to Stevens's disbelief, which indicates that when all else has gone the sound texture sustains an otherwise jeopardized lyrical dimension of poetry. Moreover, when Stevens fiddles with the idea of an *epic of disbelief*, belief in the virtues of the creative act remains, since the epic, be it of the most entertaining sort, remains a literary tradition, though revisited. Experimenting with literature is an unscathed act of the mind while metaphysics is enrolled in the poem when it is most at threat. Talking of an *epic of disbelief* remains a largely oxymoronic phrase.

Thus, Stevens produces a variety of the sublime that is of a daimonic nature,[12] one which has poetic strength and aesthetic effectiveness. The waltz ends with an unexpected celebration of shadows, which we may view as inefficient concealments of an ideal substance. The men united in these shadows perform a rite of shared experience. They symbolize togetherness and solidarity, humanism preserved within the deconstruction of the impulse to believe that the poetry produces. Beyond the awareness of the contingency of selfhood, Stevens celebrates solidarity while considering ironically the values preceding experience. Stevens the ironist is a humanist, if I can be pardoned for thus paying homage to Richard Rorty's theory of the three contingencies, respectively of language, selfhood, and the liberal community[13] (CIS 3–69).

One can argue with Richard Poirier[14] (PP 37–75) that Wallace Stevens enables the daimonic to survive in his poetry because he pays allegiance to a specific dimension of the canon of American literature, namely its linguistic skepticism, which was handed down the literary memory lane by the tradition of Emerson. Of course, Poirier's critical discussion of these issues does not assess the canonic value of this heritage, and it is quite difficult to define as a canon any set of cultural values that see language as untrustworthy. With lyrical variation of tone, Stevens, I think, clings to positive values, finding justification in poise and mood, texture and manner of expression. This is what is left of the Emersonian daimonic that Bloom tends to envisage as total, unmitigated by linguistic humility. "Our longing for the wider circumference is daimonic," Bloom tells us[15] (FCI 55), in a celebration of the Godly powers of the poet that he finds in Emerson's "Circles"[16] (EL 403–14) and makes his own.

Stevens's "Farewell to Florida" takes up again the meditations by the waters of the imagination. The mood of elation is fully preserved and its intensity carefully sustained. The narrative basis of the poem records the poet's departure from Florida, and Stevens is recapturing the moment when he left behind the Florida moon that inspired him in the writing of poetry. Can one think of any situation more apt to a celebration of lyricism? Thus says Stevens:

> Go on, high ship, since now, upon the shore,
> The snake has left its skin upon the floor.
> Key West sank downward under massive clouds
> And silvers and greens spread over the sea. The moon
> Is at the mast-head and the past is dead.
> Her mind will never speak to me again.
> I am free. High above the mast the moon
> Rides clear of her mind and the waves make a refrain
> Of this: that the snake has shed its skin upon
> The floor. Go on through the darkness. The waves fly back.
>
> (CP 117)

Is the poet the snake? Or is the poet recognizing the snake as a symbol exterior to himself? The first stanza does not make it fully clear that Stevens is leaving Florida, but we realize that

Stevens is on the way back to his home in Connecticut further down in the poem. Has the stay in Florida made the snake slough off its skin? This may explain Stevens's indication that the past is now dead while the narrator is heading back home. Stevens is adroitly poeticizing the demise of lyricism. Only with its swan song can lyricism be felt to be efficiently conveyed. Moreover, lyricism finds itself allied with the forces of evil that the snake symbolizes. The snake is part of the process of knowledge as well as a symbol of the easy sensuality of Florida, which Stevens feels are both necessary to the making of poetry. This is why the snake is both within the poet and exterior to him as a symbol; it symbolizes knowledge as the object of poetry, and poetry itself as artifact. The rhythmical variation that one finds in this poem proceeds from Stevens's uneasiness when facing Florida. The wistfulness that grows as Florida recedes in the distance causes emotional imbalance in the poet because Stevens is uncertain whether wistfulness is aesthetically acceptable as a basis for a poem. The snake is thus to be analyzed as a symbolic objectification of the author's diffidence before the emotional investment he feels he is experiencing. Similarly, and considering the sound structure in the verse, one notices a high degree of tonal instability. The underlying iambic pattern hardly pierces through, except for its strong visibility in, for example, "the snake has left its skin upon the floor," which is regular to the point of shattering the lyricism of the poem—though maybe this is intended as a necessary challenge that will help the lyrical dimension of this opening stanza to persist.

"Farewell to Florida" is a poem that raises the question of the persistence of lyricism even when emotion is extinguished. Here of course emotional extinction is threatened by the artificiality of the iambic rhythmical pattern. Elsewhere, tonal variation is also a challenge, if one understands such variation in the more general meaning of manner of expression. When one examines "Academic discourse at Havana," one realizes that the poem's emotional life comes equally, if not more systematically, under threat. Stevens, still exploring the Caribbean, produces a variety of the lyric that relies on images of decadence and the degradation of emotional life. The question at stake in this poem is whether lyricism can survive the tonal variation that the interplay of pathos and comic overtones introduces. Does lyricism, may we ask, transcend tonal differences? The poem seems to be devised to decide upon possible answers to this question:

> Canaries in the morning, orchestras
> In the afternoon, balloons at night. That is
> A difference, at least, from nightingales,
> Jehovah and the great sea-worm. The air
> Is not so elemental nor the earth
> So near.
>   But the sustenance of the wilderness
> Does not sustain us in the metropoles.
>
> (*CP* 142)

The iambic pattern has vanished; and so has the tone of seriousness of the poem, which opens negating any lyrical perspective. Stevens establishes what he calls a "difference" between the singing of the canary and the melody of the nightingale, the gloriously romantic bird. The poem is staging the conflict of the serious lyric and the amused tone. One can argue that "Academic discourse" manages to preserve lyricism at the very moment when it is undermining it. Stevens brings up the notion that our modern world is a world of "grand decadence" and the idea seems to me to redefine lyricism and thus be instrumental in making it transcend variation of tone. "A grand decadence settles down like cold," writes Stevens, announcing the reintroduction of the daimonic in the closing lines of the poem, especially with the evocation of "an infinite incantation of our selves / In the grand decadence of the perished swans." (*CP* 145)

The Tone of Social Comedy

The American critic Melita Schaum has mapped out the varying attitudes of the early critics of Stevens, who felt he was an ironist who had renounced a human perspective.[17] Many of the early critics of Stevens, Schaum insists, view Stevens's humor as subtle and "rarefied to the point it excludes a common audience." Even the burlesque, according to Laura Riding and Robert Graves, is pure clowning divorced from a sense of audience,[18] writes Schaum. One can, I think, easily demonstrate that it is unfair to overlook the sense of shared experience that goes with the clownish and the burlesque. The amused tone of most of the poems is a tone devised to be shared, because Stevens feels that it is easier to share the tone of comedy than the pathos of pure romantic lyrical expression. Moreover, Stevens may have wished to try his hand at this because he expected this variety of literary composition to free him from the anxiety of influence.

"Some friends from Pascagoula" offers amusement and solemnity in close association. Here, lyricism fares upon its negation, like metaphysics at the moment of its fall. The lilting rhythm of the ballad eases communication and facilitates the act of reading:

> Tell me more of the eagle, Cotton,
> And you, black Sly,
> Tell me how he descended
> Out of the morning sky.
>
> Describe with deepened voice
> And noble imagery
> His slowly-falling round
> Down to the fishy sea.
>
> (*CP* 126)

Stevens's voice is anything but deepened and one cannot identify any noble imagery besides the eagle's, which is contaminated by the presence of fictional heroes such as Cotton and Sly, both being of a clownish nature. These figures are akin to Hoon, the comic hero in "Sad strains of a gay waltz." Pathos rarely requires the inclusion of a fictional hero whereas serious symbolism in the ironic pieces calls for the undermining process that comes along with these anticlimactic personae. The eagle one sees here in Pascagoula symbolizes the magnitude of the poetic, which is only half-seriously condoned by Sly and Cotton, while the eagle hovers seaward, down to a *fishy* sea, one sea one may surmise to be both bizarre and nutritious to the hungry sharks. The possible sublimity the eagles were suggesting turns ridiculous. One wonders if Stevens did not at one point wish to make visible modernity's abandonment of a metaphysical perspective.

Has the interplay of social voices dried up any possible source of glorious imagery? This is what has happened and thus caused the poet's *angst*. "Lions in Sweden" (*CP* 124–25) suggested that it was the aim of poetry to capture them, also alluding to the sheer outlandishness of some of these images, easily catching on a burlesque appearance. These lions turn theatrical and the dangers of the histrionic are such that thought itself is at threat. In "Academic discourse at Havana", Stevens mentions "the toil of thought" which "evoked a peace eccentric to / The eye and tinkling to the ear." Is not this tinkling reminiscent of the bells of the jester? Thought itself seems to have been turned inside

out and the poem's inner space to be open to public display, so
that privacy has now gone. The poets' ego is caught in otherness,
which is a new area of lyrical expression for Stevens, while being
the outcome of the play of social voices within the poetry. This
is why the poet has no angel left, as the very title "Evening
without angels" indicates. No transcendence is possible except
if thought can be shared and if it is based on communicative
reason, rather than subject-centered reason, if we refer to the
well-known Habermas distinction.[19] Yet an inner angel, though
unnamed, is preserved and survives Stevens's overriding
skepticism:

> Bare night is best. Bare earth is best. Bare, bare,
> Except for our own houses, huddled low
> Beneath the arches and their spangled air,
> Beneath the rhapsodies of fire and fire,
> Where the voice that is in us makes a true response,
> Where the voice that is great within us rises up,
> As we stand gazing at the rounded moon.
>
> (CP 137–38)

The poet feels there is substance in this voice—both angelic and
demonic. Stevens has reconciled with the moon, which embodies a symbol of circularity. Stevens's moon is here rounded,
which is a tautological expression aiming at special emphasis,
as nobody would expect the moon to be square or rectangular.
Circularity in Stevens is a celebration of community. Stanza
three mentions the wind encircling a group of men and one will
also remember the supple and turbulent ring of men chanting
"in orgy on a summer morn / Their boisterous devotion to the
sun" in "Sunday Morning". These circles, indeed the highly Emersonian circles of an expanding consciousness,[20] are the circles
of thought and poetry reaching in conjunction, for truths that
can be communicated though they proceed from the subject.
I think Stevens adumbrates one of the findings of Pragmatist
philosopher of language Donald Davidson who once stated that
"a creature cannot have thoughts unless it is the interpreter of
the words of another."[21] Stevens is not, however, giving us any
particular example of these truths as maybe he believes it is not
the business of poetry to be doing so. Yet his self-introspection
celebrates the communal dimension of art, language and
thought, providing us with a lesson that has the ambition of
transcending the merely aesthetic scope of the poem. One might
at this point argue that metaphysics only serves to harden the

bedrock on which it is quietly sitting. The words spoken in "Evening without angels" are always, wittingly or unwittingly, the words of another:

> Let this be clear that we are men of sun
> And men of day and never of pointed night,
> Men that repeat antiquest sounds of air
> In an accord of repetitions. Yet,
> If we repeat, it is because the wind
> Encircling us, speaks always with our speech.
>
> (*CP* 137)

The men encircled by the wind reject the words of other men and women that speak through them. This is why they give credit to their unconvincing vision of being men of the sun, not spoken through by the dead that would visit them if they were men of night, when consciousness does not censor the unconscious dimension of language. One finds a further illusion in their belief that the wind speaks using their speech, because it is words spoken by another that come to their lips. The process of reinterpreting another's language feeds their illusion that they are the only talkers. Stevens, thinking about his own poetry, would like to remain unaware of being spoken through by a whole tradition. Very much as Emerson had done—this, we may think, is where the literary and the philosophical inspiration comes from in a great deal of Stevens's writings—the need to forget oneself proceeds from the idea that the circle of one's consciousness should be expanded, as is implied in "Circles." The need to expand one's awareness may also be felt to proceed from the fear of memory, which may at times bind you to a heritage and threaten your apparent integrity. Emerson is clear on this: "The one thing which we seek with insatiable desire is to forget ourselves, to be surprised out of our propriety, to lose our sempiternal memory, and to do something without knowing how or why; in short, to draw a new circle."[22] Amnesia is misleading to Stevens, though he is willing to play the game of forgetting, while one can suggest that amnesia was to Emerson a temptation that went with a literary nationalism to which he subscribed enthusiastically.

All in all, studying variation of tone in Stevens's poetry leads to a general critical examination of some of the key issues the poet faced as a maker of his world. Differences in tone however

are related to results so estranged from what inspired them—
redefining lyricism, opposing metronomic verse, accepting otherness—that they cannot be said to grow from the author's intention unscathed by the challenge of drafting and redrafting
poems. One can say that Stevens started out with a strategy that
consisted in producing one renewed form of lyricism that involved variation of tone and that he grew aware that the difference one encounters in writing is the one separating the poem
from the intention that gives it life.

Notes

1. "Stevens without Epistemology," in *Wallace Stevens: The Poetics of Modernism,* ed. Albert Gelpi (New York: Cambridge University Press, 1985), 24–40.
2. Charles Altieri, *Painterly Abstraction in Modernist American Poetry.
The Contemporaneity of Modernism* (New York: Cambridge University Press,
1989), 327.
3. Jürgen Habermas, *The Philosophical Discourse of Modernism,* trans.
Frederick Lawrence (Cambridge, Mass.: Polity Press, 1987), 161–84.
4. Richard Poirier, *Poetry and Pragmatism* (Cambridge, Mass., and London: Harvard University Press and Faber, 1992), 31.
5. Timothy Steele, *Missing Measures. Modern Poetry and the Revolt
Against Meter* (Fayetteville and London: The University of Arkansas Press,
1990), 59–60.
6. Wallace Stevens, *Collected Poems* (Boston and London: Faber, 1955),
128. Hereafter abridged to *CP.*
7. Harold Bloom, *Wallace Stevens. The Poems of Our Climate* (Ithaca and
London: Cornell University Press, 1976), 88.
8. Helen Vendler, *Wallace Stevens. Words Chosen Out Of Desire* (Cambridge, Mass., and London: Harvard University Press, 1984), 68.
9. Richard Poirier, *Poetry,* 3–33.
10. "Experience," in Ralph Waldo Emerson, *Essays and Lectures,* ed. Joel
Porte (New York: The Library of America, 1983), 486.
11. Elizabeth A. Frost, "Revisions of Romanticism in *Notes toward a Supreme Fiction,*" *The Wallace Stevens Journal* 15, 1 (1991), 37–54.
12. Cf. Rob Wilson, *American Sublime. The Genealogy of a Poetic Genre*
(Madison: The University of Wisconsin Press, 1991), 169–96.
13. Richard Rorty, *Contingency, Irony and Solidarity* (New York: Cambridge University Press, 1989), 3–69.
14. Richard Poirier, *Poetry,* 37–75.
15. Harold Bloom, *Figures of Capable Imagination* (New York: The Seabury
Press, 1976).
16. Ralph Waldo Emerson, *Experience,* 403–14.
17. Melita Schaum, "Concepts of Irony in Wallace Stevens' Early Critics,"
The Wallace Stevens Journal 9, 2 (1985), 85–97.
18. Ibid., 93.
19. Jürgen Habermas, *Discourse,* 294–326.
20. Ralph Waldo Emerson, *Experience,* 403–14.

21. "Thought and Talk" in Donald Davidson, *Inquiries into Truth and Interpretation* (New York: The Clarendon Press of Oxford University Press, 1984), 157.
22. Ralph Waldo Emerson, *Experience,* 414.

Works Cited

Altieri, Charles. *Painterly Abstraction in Modernist American Poetry; The Contemporaneity of Modernism*. Cambridge and New York: Cambridge University Press, 1989.

Bloom, Harold. *Wallace Stevens; The Poems of Our Climate*. Ithaca and London: Cornell University Press, 1976.

————. *Figures of Capable Imagination*. New York: The Seabury Press, 1976.

Davidson, Donald. *Inquiries into Truth and Interpretation*. Oxford and New York: The Clarendon Press of Oxford University Press, 1984.

Emerson, Ralph Waldo. *Essays and Lectures*. ed. Joel Porte. New York: The Library of America, 1983.

Frost, Elizabeth A. "Revisions of Romanticism in *Notes toward a Supreme Fiction*." *The Wallace Stevens Journal* 15.1 (1991): 37–54.

Gelpi, Albert, ed. *Wallace Stevens: The Poetics of Modernism*. Cambridge and New York: Cambridge University Press, 1985.

Habermas, Jürgen. *The Philosophical Discourse of Modernism*, trans. Frederick Lawrence. Cambridge, Mass.: Polity Press, 1987.

Poirier, Richard. *Poetry and Pragmatism*. Cambridge, Mass., and London: Harvard University Press and Faber, 1992.

Rorty, Richard. *Contingency, Irony and Solidarity*. Cambridge and New York: Cambridge University Press, 1989.

Schaum, Melita. "Concepts of Irony in Wallace Stevens's Early Critics." *The Wallace Stevens Journal* 9.2 (1985) : 85–97.

Steele, Timothy. *Missing Measures; Modern Poetry and the Revolt Against Meter*. Fayetteville and London: The University of Arkansas Press, 1990.

Stevens, Wallace. *Collected Poems*. Boston and London: Faber, 1955.

Vendler, Helen. *Wallace Stevens; Words Chosen Out Of Desire*. Cambridge, Mass., and London: Harvard University Press, 1984.

Wilson, Rob. *American Sublime; the Genealogy of a Poetic Genre*. Madison and London: The University of Wisconsin Press, 1991.

Wallace Stevens and Jean Wahl

On a stormy day in Paris, eighteen years to the day of the death of Jean Wahl in 1974, his daughter Beatrice gave me the manuscript of the poems her father had written in English during the Second World War at Mount Holyoke College.[1] Together, we opened the black binding, which had a dusty feel to it, and turned the pages, on which, very often, there were only three or four lines of poetry typed on a wafer-thin paper, which bore silent witness to wartime restrictions. We laughed together at the idea that Jean Wahl would have been happy to see us discovering together his poem *Four Anti Quartets,* both an echo of and an answer to T. S. Eliot's recently published *Four Quartets* as well as the poems "Minute Particulars" and "Toward the Concrete," which by their titles, form, and content revealed just as deep a knowledge of the poetry of Wallace Stevens. The double interest of Jean Wahl for the Anglo-American Eliot and the American Stevens was all the more astonishing, as the two poets had a conception of the nature of reality and therefore of poetry, which were diametrically opposed to one another. Toward the end of his life, Wallace Stevens took pains to point out that there was nothing in common with his manner of writing poetry and Eliot's: "After all, Eliot and I are dead opposites and I have been doing about everything that he would not be likely to do."[2] The dissimilitude between the conceptions of Stevens and Eliot about the nature of reality could not have failed to interest the philosopher and poet Jean Wahl, author of *Vers le concret* (1932) and *Rôle de l'instant dans l'oeuvre de Descartes,* (1920), who had been stripped of his professorship at the Sorbonne and sent to a concentration camp at Drancy outside Paris before escaping to become a professor in exile at Mount Holyoke.

The story of Jean Wahl and Wallace Stevens is a complex one, that of a warm and lasting friendship cloaking a longstanding difference of opinion concerning the nature of poetry, which the daring strategy of Stevens in his Pontigny essay "The Figure of the Youth As Virile Poet"—a mixture of provocation and reverence—did not manage to overcome. Although he failed to convince Jean Wahl that reality contained everything contained in the imagination, the essay of Stevens remains a landmark in his attempt to define a new concept of the nature of reality and therefore of poetry, one that he would perhaps not have written without the stimulus of Jean Wahl's invitation to the *Entretiens de Pontigny* held at Mount Holyoke in 1943. Until recently, the answer of Jean Wahl to Wallace Stevens has escaped notice, but it was both immediate and very forceful, as we shall see.

Stevens chose for the *Entretiens de Pontigny* an apparently banal topic "The Poet and His Art," a title that was actually printed on the program and that hid completely the revolutionary nature of his paper, the "intimidating thesis" that "absolute fact includes everything that the imagination includes."[3] By containing the imagination within the perception of reality, Stevens rejected the omnipresent domination of the imagination that had existed in poetry since the beginning of the nineteenth century. Stevens quoted Coleridge, the eminent theoretician of the imagination, as the author of definitions that were no longer relevant in the twentieth century: ". . . a man who may be said to have been defining poetry all his life in definitions that are valid enough but which no longer impress us primarily by their validity."[4]

Stevens indicated the importance of his rupture with the Romantic past by choosing a title, "The Figure of the Youth as Virile Poet," that brings immediately to mind the painting of Marcel Duchamp exhibited at the Armory Show of 1913, *Jeune homme triste dans un train* (1911). Duchamp's painting was one of a number that had revealed new aesthetic possibilities to the young generation of American poets. William Carlos Williams described the impact of the Armory Show as an electrifying moment that gave new hope and inspiration to the young men and women who were attempting to write a typically American poetry, a moment of hope that according to Williams, was cut short with the publication of T. S. Eliot's poem *The Waste Land* in 1922:

> Those were the years just before the great catastrophe to our letters—the appearance of T. S. Eliot's *The Waste Land*. There was heat in us, a core and a drive that was gathering headway upon the theme of a rediscovery of a primary impetus, the elementary principle of all art, in the local conditions. Our work staggered to a halt for a

moment under the blast of Eliot's genius which gave the poem back to the academics. We did not know how to answer him.[5]

The disappointment of Williams was, as he himself stated, that of an entire generation of young poets who had spent hours discussing the aesthetic implications of cubism with the circle of Walter Arensberg, a personal friend of Stevens from Harvard days: "We'd have arguments over cubism which would fill an afternoon. There was a comparable whipping up of interest in the structure of a poem."[6] Although it is well known that William Carlos Williams spent his poetic lifetime searching for the means to give an adequate response to T. S. Eliot, it has perhaps never been recognized that Wallace Stevens also spent his poetic lifetime trying to find an answer to the Anglo-American who had given poetry back to an elite.

Through his allusion to the Armory Show, to a painter whom he knew personally and to his own beginning years as a poet, Stevens implicitly suggested to his international audience at Pontigny both the initial enthusiasm and disappointed hope of the years immediately following the Armory Show. In his use of painting to create the portrait of an ideal poet to which he adds allusions to the work of Jean Wahl, Stevens rendered homage to Wahl himself:

> We have been referring constantly to the simple figure of the youth, in his character of poet, as virile poet. . . . As we say these things, there begins to develop, in addition to the figure that has been seated in our midst, composed in the radiant and productive atmosphere with which we have surrounded him, an intimation of what he is thinking as the reflects on the imagination of life determined to be its master and ours.[7]

The tribute to Jean Wahl is coupled with what seems to be a direct attack upon philosophy and philosophers, a strange strategy if we take into account the philosophical origin of the *Entretiens* themselves—invited under the Presidence of Jacques Maritain were Claude Levi-Strauss, Paul Weiss, Suzanne Langer, Alexandre Koyre, James B. Pratt, Raymond de Saussure—and the fact that Stevens had been invited by one of the foremost philosophers among them, Jean Wahl.

It has long been a source of wonder that Jean Wahl never directly answered the affirmations of Stevens that the end of philosophy is despair and the end of poetry joy, that the idea of

God is uniquely poetic and has no relation to philosophy, that poetry is a nonofficial view of being opposed to philosophy, the official view of being.[8] We know today that Jean Wahl did answer Wallace Stevens, although without naming him, in an article entitled "On Poetry" published in *The Chimera*'s winter-spring issue of 1944, four months after the *Entretiens de Pontigny*:

> Here we might reflect on the possible union of poetry and philosophy. For it is, perhaps, or so we hope, not completely true to oppose poetry as unofficial view of being. Philosophers have very often emphasized the importance of immediate and poetic knowledge.[9]

In the French version of the text, which is a translation of the original, Stevens is mentioned by name.

> Dans une belle conférence, Wallace Stevens a soutenu que la poésie est une vue non officielle de l'être tandis que la philosophie en est la vue officielle. Mais pourquoi cette opposition ? Bien des philosophes n'ont-ils pas maintenu l'importance de la connaissance immédiate en poétique ?[10]

The two texts of Jean Wahl are identical except for the addition of the name of Stevens in the French version. Why did Jean Wahl choose not to answer Stevens directly at the *Entretiens,* not to mention him in the article published in the United States, and to quote him only in the French version, which Stevens was unlikely to read?

Silence Versus Light

We know today that the Stevens's conference had moved Jean Wahl deeply enough to write his own magnificent conception of the nature of reality and of poetry, which ends with a definition based on the infinite vibrations of silence:

> Perhaps we could say that the poetry is only our manner of giving hues and vibrations to the silence by which the poem is followed and enveloped.[11]

In his discourse, at the *Entretiens,* Wallace Stevens had spoken of a kind of vibration of forms absorbed by their own light:

> The acute intelligence of the imagination, the illimitable resources of its memory, its power to possess the moment it perceives—if we

were speaking of light itself, and thinking of the relationship between objects and light, no further demonstration would be necessary. Like light, it adds nothing but itself. What light requires a day to do, and by day I mean a kind of Biblical revolution of time, the imagination does in the twinkling of an eye. It colors, increases, brings to a beginning and end, invents languages, crushes men and, for that matter, gods in its hands . . .[12]

Light, of course, is the destructive element in cubist painting which allows the infinite multiplication of the instant and of space into innumerable refractions and mirrors of itself, which deforms an object so that other forms can exist. As Guillaume Appolinaire had insisted in his study *Les Poètes Cubistes,* light was at the base of the new technique: *De même, les peintres nouveaux procurent à leurs admirateurs des sensations artistiques uniquement dues à l'harmonie des lumières impaires*[13] or: *J'aime l'art d'aujourd'hui parce que j'aime avant tout la lumière*[14] or: *La flamme est le symbole de la peinture et les trois vertus plastiques flambent en rayonnant.*[15] By adhering to the aesthetic tenets of the cubist painters whom he had met in the circle of Walter Arensberg, not only Duchamp but Francis Picabia and the critic Albert Gleizes, Stevens was advocating the adoption of a new concept of reality in poetry. Because it is unlikely that he ever read Jean Wahl's *Sur la poésie,* Stevens probably never realized how successful his double strategy of provocation and tribute had been in capturing and retaining the attention of Jean Wahl, who, if he did not agree with the proposals of Stevens, at least took them seriously enough to write his own remarkable answer. Let us take a closer look at the double strategy of Stevens at the *Entretiens de Pontigny* held at Mt. Holyoke in August 1943.

The Strategy of Provocation

Stevens opened his paper "The Figure of the Youth as Virile Poet" by indirectly indicating his skepticism with regard to the value of philosophy in general, using a quotation from Henry Bradley: ". . . I feel that the universe of being is too vast to be comprehended even by the greatest of the sons of Adam"[16] and by scrupulously avoiding any direct criticism of his own. Stevens followed with references to two personal friends of Jean Wahl, the philosopher Henri Bergson and the poet Paul Valéry. In fact,

Stevens used a quotation from Valéry to suggest that the work of Bergson was becoming obsolete and outmoded : *Bergson semble déjà appartenir à un âge révolu, et son nom est le dernier grand nom de l'histoire de l'intelligence européenne.*[17] As he continued reading his paper, the implacable rhetoric of Stevens allowed philosophers to condemn themselves out of their own mouths. The American philosopher William James, to whom Jean Wahl had devoted three long articles in his book *Vers le concret,* is quoted by Stevens as saying:

> Many philosophers have been invalid—I too am one of those, I cannot sleep, make a decision, buy a horse, all the things which ordinary men do.[18]

In what is an unusal assertion for the time, that of the inevitable intermingling of the literary and philosophic genres, Stevens quotes a letter sent by William James to Henri Bergson after reading Bergson's work *L'Evolution créatrice* : "You may be amused at the comparison, but in finishing it I found the same aftertaste remaining as after finishing *Madame Bovary,* such a flavor of persistent euphony."[19]

By setting the stage for a debate, Stevens had done no more than bow to the initial demand of Jean Wahl, who had specifically asked him to give a paper that would generate discussion. In a letter to Wahl, Stevens indicated that he wrote the paper with this aim in mind : "Since it might be helpful, by way of promoting discussion, for me to send you a copy or two of my paper before it is read, I shall be glad to do this if you wish it."[20] What Stevens had intended as matter for discussion must have appeared so excessive to Jean Wahl as he listened to Stevens that he preferred to avoid a discussion of the paper's most pertinent aspects. This hypothesis is confirmed by the reaction of Paul Weiss, who admitted years later to Peter Brazeau that although he admired Stevens, he had been shocked in reading the printed version of "The Figure of the Youth As Virile Poet." He said that he had been shocked by what Stevens had said, especially by the manner in which Henri Bergson had been treated:

> I thought, now, here's a man saying some important things. I thought very highly of him, and I wanted him to see : now, what were you going to do if you get a real full-sized philosopher who's making a great contribution, one of the great historic figures ? Are

you going to speak in a derogatory way of him, as you did of Bergson?"[21]

According to Paul Weiss, there should have been a violent reaction, if not from Jean Wahl, then from members of the audience, but none followed in spite of the fact that Stevens had given the example of the honorary president of the *Entretiens*, M. Jacques Maritain, as a model not to be imitated: " . . . in spite of M. Jacques Maritain, we do not want to become metaphysicians."[22] Not only was Stevens not perceived as an outrageous rebel, he gave the impression of being a dignified, shy, and reserved poet. Constance de Saintonge, professor at Mount Holyoke saw in Stevens not only a soothing presence but an angelic one: "He was like an angel who flew in for a moment and went out."[23] If we take into consideration the very different reactions of the members of the audience, we must conclude that the words of Stevens were not understood and that Jean Wahl did nothing to shed light on the subject. This hypothesis is confirmed by Stevens's account of the proceedings at Mount Holyoke in a letter to Hi Simons:

> For the most part the members of the audience were French who spoke English as well as I speak French. When I had finished, Jean Wahl made a resume in French of what I had said. It was followed by a discussion in English during which I answered all the questions in English.[24]

The debate on the nature of reality and the imagination, which should have been a heated one, was apparently calm to the point of being dull and uninteresting, due to the prudence and diplomacy of Jean Wahl, who preferred to reserve his answer for another tribune.

Homage Rendered To Jean Wahl

The reserved attitude of Jean Wahl is all the more surprising, as he was renowned for his ability to immediately detect the controversial or weak point of any argument with which he did not agree: . . . *il n'avait pas son pareil pour toucher le point faible, formuler l'objection imparable.*[25] The fact that he did not answer Wallace Stevens immediately is an indication that he did recognize the tribute of Stevens. By speaking even in a critical manner of philosophers close to Jean Wahl, Stevens was addressing himself directly to Wahl and to no one else; it would seem that the paper "The Figure of the Youth as Virile Poet" was intended to be a debate between the two men. From Jean Wahl's answer in his essay "On Poetry" we know that he was perfectly aware of the importance of Stevens's remarks about the nature of reality and poetic inspiration. Jean Wahl must have recognized as well excerpts from his own exchange of letters with Stevens on subject of *refacimento* and its importance in any consideration of the nature of fiction and reality:

> After having defined poetic truth as the truth of reality, because reality includes poetic reality, that is to say the unlimited number of real things which are like the objects of the imagination, and after having rid the imagination of all that is unnecessary, we can turn once again to the figure of the youth as virile poet.[26]

In a letter to Henry Church, Wallace Stevens had shared the response of Jean Wahl to his volume of poetry *Notes Toward a Supreme Fiction*: "At first I attempted to follow a scheme, and the first poem bore the caption *REFACIMENTO*. Jean Wahl picked that up right off. The first step toward a supreme fiction would be to get rid of all existing fictions. A thing stands out in clear air better than it does in soot."[27]

It is also quite likely that Jean Wahl was able, after teaching philosophy in the United States, to place Stevens's paper in the context of a time when philosophy was considered, especially by philosophers and also by many poets, to be a noble discipline to which poetry was of secondary or tributary importance. He would certainly have realized that Stevens's desire not to become a metaphysician 'in spite of Jacques Maritain' was not so much an attack as a matter of poetic self-defense. Because he was himself working on the *Four Anti Quartets,* he was aware of the importance of the concept of time in its philosophical sense for T. S. Eliot in his *Four Quartets,* which had been published to wide acclaim on May 12, 1943. It is probable that Jean Wahl recognized the attempt of Stevens to differentiate his poetry as well as his theory of poetry from that of Eliot. The differences existing between the expatriate American poets and those who had remained at home constituted another very sensitive subject, best not discussed perhaps in the atmosphere of the *Entretiens.* If we can judge from his answer, what must have seemed most serious, however, in the eyes of Jean Wahl were Stevens's arguments that reduced the importance of the imagination. From an uncontrollable, independent element outside the range of human consciousness, it had simply become part of reality. Stevens condemned the idea of the imagination as an uncontrollable force: "... the false conception of the imagination like an unfathomable oracle in us."[28] In his answer to Stevens in the article "On poetry," Jean Wahl felt obliged to defend both the imagination and the subconscious in poetic intercourse: "To be a poet is to have the consciousness of one's unconsciousness. It is the accomplishing of a movement from unconsciousness to consciousness. We see this movement in Valery and T. S. Eliot as in the Surrealist."[29] The text of Jean Wahl is an ardent defense of the imagination springing from the unconscious, the inexhaustible substrata of poetry, which Wahl recognized in many poets. In this category, the name of Wallace Stevens is not mentioned.

At Mount Holyoke, Stevens must have felt that his strategy of provocation and tribute had failed. He probably did not know that his arguments were directed at the major interest of Jean Wahl at the time or that Jean Wahl was writing his own poem about the nature of reality in answer to Eliot's *Four Quartets,* lines with which Stevens would have agreed:

> But you cannot blot out the present
> Which first you so highly praised
> We are of this place and this time,
> Indelibly.
>
> *Four Anti Quartets,* Little Gidding V[30]

Stevens would also have been delighted if he had read Wahl's poem "Minute Particulars," which conveys Wahl's belief that it is the singularity of objects that allows the poet to re-create the effect of reality, that infinite details are the source of the greatest joys in poetry, that generalities, like soot, hide the earth and give it a devastated aspect:

> In this country desertio
> Where future dust mirages itself into soft flowers
> We shall find nothing but mere generality.
> And nowhere the pure inexhaustible individual,
> Nowhere the source divine.
> The tree of reality fades into dust.[31]

If, as is likely, Stevens had not read the poems, he knew of their existence. In a letter to Stevens in 1945, Wahl mentions going to see the publisher Alfred Knopf in New York with a recommendation from Stevens and submitting his manuscript of English poems with a view to publication.[32] The fact that Wahl was writing poetry in English was in fact an open secret. An article on Jean Wahl written by Basso Hamilton, which appeared in *The New Yorker* magazine on 12 May 1945 also mentions the fact that Wahl has "enough poems written in English to fill a book."[33] We do not yet know how close Stevens was to the poems of Wahl, whether his interest was one of friendship only or if he had been asked to read them and to give his opinion of them.

When Wahl returned to France, the correspondence with Stevens continued; Madame Jean Wahl remembers meeting Stevens with her husband in New York after the war.[34] There is a very interesting exchange of letters at the time when Stevens was collecting material for his discourse "The Collect of Philosophy" in which he was to state once again that poetry was superior to philosophy. At the time, Stevens confided to Barbara Church that Wahl had not really understood the relationship that he was trying to develop between philosophy and poetry: "However, like another correspondent, he answered somewhat on the relations between poetry and philosophy, which is not what I want. What I want is to take advantage of his endless reading of philosophy to identify instances of philosophic concepts not in the least intended to be poetic which are poetic in spite of themselves. Then, too, both men seem to think that I am specializing in phases of perception, which is merely an instance. I have written to Jean Wahl trying to be more precise . . ."[35]

It would seem that both Jean Wahl and Wallace Stevens kept steadfastly to their respective positions over the years while remaining on very friendly terms. The young French philosopher Frederic Worms may have explained better than anyone else some of the reasons for the differences that existed between Stevens and Wahl. Frederic Worms indicates that Wahl bases his philosophical arguments on the Bergsonian concept of the image. By relating the Bergsonian concept of the image to the concept of the imagination of Schelling and Coleridge as well as to neoplatonic philosophers, Jean Wahl presents a theory of poetry as a unity of symbolic terms in the finished work of the imagination.[36] These are exactly the arguments that Stevens was trying to refute at Mount Holyoke in 1943, arguments that Wahl resisted and that he felt obliged to answer emphatically in his article "On Poetry."

Another point of probable difference between Stevens and Wahl is their conception of time. Wahl's complementary thesis of 1920, *Le rôle de l'idée de l'instant dans la philosophie de Descartes* is dedicated to Henri Bergson, from whom Wahl's concept of time originates. Basically, time is an indivisible unit: *"l'intuition qui saisit d'un seul regard, la lumière qui se meut d'un même branle, Dieu qui crée et conserve par son action unique."*[37] Stevens's concept that light destroys this unity in order to present its innumerable refractions may have gone against the foundation of the thought of Jean Wahl. Frederic Worms reminds us as well that Jean Wahl and T. S. Eliot could have been students together at the Sorbonne when Henri Bergson lectured in 1910. Although both Jean Wahl and T. S. Eliot may have taken their concepts of time in part fron the teaching of Bergson, their concepts are not identical, for Jean Wahl takes issue in *Four Anti Quartets* with Eliot's conception of time:

> And I don't like so much the mixture of present, past, future,
> Of end and beginning,
> Of eternity and time,
> When they are so ill defined,
> And the intention of cause immovable,
> And the exclusion of hope,
> Except the hope of resignation
>
> *Four Anti Quartets,* Little Gidding V [38]

If Wahl disagreed with Stevens on the nature of reality and the imagination, he also disagreed with T. S. Eliot's conception of time as an eternal present in the *Four Quartets*.[39] Wahl's answer to Eliot is just as forceful as his answer to Stevens.

According to Frederic Worms, there is another instance in which Jean Wahl agreed with Henri Bergson, and that could have prevented him from agreeing with Stevens on the nature of reality and the imagination. Wahl, like Bergson, believed in the idea of a separation between the idea and the thing considered, a distance that is that of signification, a concept that led him to write the following lines in the poem *Dialogue*: *"Jouir de l'être, sentant qu'être n'est rien qu'un verbe. / Aimer le vent, le sol, flairer l'odeur de l'herbe, voir toutes les couleurs, puis entrer dans le noir."*[40] Language seemed to be a symbolic concept in the eyes of Jean Wahl, while Stevens believed that language was part of reality. It is difficult to imagine Wallace Stevens accepting Wahl's definition of being as a simple verb or to imagine him accepting Wahl's idea of the progression of reality toward darkness.

Frederic Worms has also identified a point of interest and junction in the work of the two men that they probably did not realize they shared. When he returned to France after the war, Jean Wahl taught a course on Van Gogh at the Sorbonne. Frederic Worms has qualified his remarks on Van Gogh in *L'Expérience métaphysique* published in 1953 as the culminating point of his argument, for Wahl insists that Van Gogh is a "source of philosophy": *C'est celui-là, mon Dieu, le plus proche de moi, / saint fou dans les champs d'oliviers de Provence, / Navré, porté au ciel par sa grande souffrance.*[41]

It is in the passage from the eye to the spirit, in the moment of transmission from eye to spirit that reality comes into existence for Jean Wahl. The privilege of Van Gogh is to show and to say simultaneously.[42]

In a letter written in 1943 to Henry Church, Wallace Stevens insisted that Van Gogh had accomplished the total subjection of reality to his art: " . . . the word for all this is maniement; I don't mean a mania of matter, but I mean the total subjection of reality to the artist." It may be only too true that Van Gogh had fortuitous assistance in the mastery of reality. But he mastered it, no matter how. And that is so often what one wants to do in poetry, to seize the whole mass of everything and squeeze it and make it one's own. When the philosophical arguments were removed Wallace Stevens and Jean Wahl perhaps agreed more completely than either realized on the essential quality of art and poetry.

Notes

1. The quotations from the poems of Jean Wahl are printed with the permission of Béatrice Wahl. Part of the text was printed in another form in *Jean Wahl, le poète, in'hui, Le cri,* vol. 39, (Bruxelles: December, 1992). Information on the *Entretiens de Pontigny* was kindly supplied by Patricia Albright of the Mount Holyoke College Archives.

2. Wallace Stevens, *Collected Letters,* ed. Holly Stevens (New York: Alfred Knopf, 1981), no. 737, April 25, 1950, 677.

3. Wallace Stevens, "The Figure of the Youth As Virile Poet," in *The Necessary Angel* (London and Boston: Faber, 1960), 61.

4. Ibid., 41.

5. William Carlos Williams, *Autobiography* (New York: Random House, 1948), 146.

6. Ibid., 136.

7. "The Figure of the Youth As Virile Poet," *Necessary*, 60.

8. Ibid., 51, 42, 45, 59.

9. Jean Wahl, "On Poetry," *Chimera*, vol. 2, no. 3, (winter-spring, 1944).

10. "Sur la poésie," ibid.

11. "On Poetry," *Chimera*, 41.

12. "The Figure of the Youth As Virile Poet," *Necessary*, 61–62.

13. Guillaume Apollinaire, *Les Peintres Cubistes*, (Paris: Hermann, 1980), 59.

14. Ibid., 130.

15. Ibid., 54.

16. "The Figure of the Youth As Virile Poet," *Necessary*, 39.

17. Ibid.

18. Ibid., 58–59.

19. Ibid., 40.

20. Wallace Stevens, *Collected Letters*, no. 481, 9 April 1943, 447.

21. Peter Brazeau, *Parts of a World, Wallace Stevens Remembered*, Random House, New York, 185.

22. "The Figure of the Youth As Virile Poet," *Necessary*, 59.

23. Peter Brazeau, *Parts*, 184.

24. Wallace Stevens, *Collected Letters*, no. 494, 11 October 1943, 457.

25. Xavier de Tilliette, "Portrait de Jean Wahl," *Archives de Philosophie*, 37, (octobre-décembre, 1974), 530.

26. "The Figure of the Youth As Virile Poet," *Necessary*, 62.

27. Wallace Stevens, *Collected Letters*, no. 467, 8 December 1942, 431.

28. "The Figure of the Youth As Virile Poet," *Necessary*, 61.

29. Jean Wahl, "On Poetry," *Chimera*, 35.

30. Manuscript of Jean Wahl, 202.

31. Ibid., 278.

32. Jean Wahl, unpublished letter to Stevens at the Huntington dated 13 June 1944. The Huntington Library.

33. *The New Yorker,* 12 May 1945, 27.

34. Conversation with Béatrice Wahl, 19 June 1992.

35. Wallace Stevens, *Collected Letter,* no. 796, 15 August 1951, 725.

36. Frederic Worms, "Jean Wahl vers lui-même," *in'hui*, no. 39, 108.

37. Jean Wahl quoted in Frederic Worms, *Jean Wahl*, 102.

38. Jean Wahl, *Little Gidding V,* 203.

39. Frederic Worms, *Jean Wahl*, 100.

40. Jean Wahl quoted in Frederic Worms, *Jean Wahl*, 107.

41. Frederic Worms, *Jean Wahl*, 119–20.

42. Ibid.

(Dys)functionings of Difference: The Intertext at Work in Theodore Roethke's "Four for Sir John Davies"

AXEL NESME

The Poet Listening to the Dead

ROETHKE GAVE A FULL ACCOUNT IN HIS THEORETICAL WRITINGS OF the circumstances surrounding the composition of "The Dance," the first poem of this sequence (published in *The Waking* in 1953), and I would like to quote him by way of introduction:

> Let me say boldly, now, that the extent to which the great dead can be evoked, or can come to us, can be eerie, and astonishing. Let me, at the risk of seeming odd, recite a personal incident.
>
> I was in that particular hell of the poet: a longish dry period. It was 1952, I was 44, and I thought I was done. I was living alone in a biggish house in Edmonds, Washington. I had been reading—and re-reading—not Yeats, but Ralegh and Sir John Davies. I had been teaching the five-beat line for weeks—I knew quite a bit about it, but write it myself?—*no :* so I felt myself a fraud.
>
> Suddenly, in the early evening, the poem "The Dance" started, and finished itself in a very short time—say thirty minutes, maybe in the greater part of an hour, it was all done. I felt, I *knew,* I had hit it. I walked around, and I wept; and I knelt down—I always do after I've written what I know is a good piece. But at the same time I had, as God is my witness, the actual sense of a Presence—as if Yeats himself were *in* that room. The experience was in a way terrifying, for it lasted at least half an hour. That house, I repeat, was charged with a psychic presence: the very walls seemed to shimmer. I wept for joy. At last I was somebody again. He, they—the poets dead—were with me.
>
> Now I know there are any number of cynical explanations for this phenomenon: auto-suggestion, the unconscious playing an elaborate trick, and so on, but I accept none of them. It was one of the most profound experiences of my life.[1]

87

As we can see, Roethke is anxious to acknowledge his indebtedness to dead poets. To this extent he conceives of the writing process along the same lines as T. S. Eliot in his most famous essay:

> No poet, no artist of any art, has his complete meaning alone. His significance, his appreciation is the appreciation of his relation to the dead poets and artists. You cannot value him alone; you must set him for contrast and comparison, among the dead. I mean this as a principle of aesthetic, not merely historical criticism. The necessity that he shall conform, that he shall cohere, is not one-sided; what happens when a new work of art is created is something that happens simultaneously to all the works of art which preceded it. The existing monuments form an ideal order among themselves, which is modified by the introduction of the new (the really new) work of art among them.[2]

Although Roethke never cared much for Eliot, whose concern with the "perpetual extinction of personality" he certainly did not share, several of his notebook entries do testify to what degree he had appropriated Eliot's reflections on the poet's necessary relationship to his literary forefathers. Thus, Roethke writes about himself: "In him all the oafs, dolts, bumpkins, and clods, living and dead connect and contend."[3] The poetic ego is identified here as a locus where texts circulate and meet; he is open not only to comparison, but essentially to the speech of the Other. Indeed, as the reader of "Four for Sir John Davies" soon finds out, the poem intersects the voices of Shakespeare, Yeats, Dante, and Sir John Davies himself, which Roethke puts in resonance the better to make us hear, though sometimes with mixed success, the voice of his own desire.

The title of the sequence sets up a particular situation of communication whose terms I would like to pin down. Writing "Four for Sir John Davies," means positing an "I," that of the author of the title, a "you," that of the reader[4], and finally a "he," namely the Elizabethan poet: to *him*, I, the author, tell *you*, my reader, that these texts are dedicated. It thus seems, to quote Emile Benvéniste's terminology, that the addressee is split between a person and a nonperson in this poem written to the living, yet *for* a dead man, and also split, I would venture to say, between the other and the capitalized Other. In this communication scheme, Sir John Davies functions as the absent Other whose voice the subject of the statement indirectly brings into resonance in an attempt to make us hear the subject of *utterance,* via the play of textual difference. The intertextual strategy at work here thus seeks to open itself to the speech of the Other, an undertaking whose success is never guaranteed, so great is the risk of freezing the intertext into erudite quoting.

Why, however, choose Sir John Davies, this philosopher-poet who was anthologized if not among the "lesser," then among the "silver" poets of the sixteenth century? Perhaps because, much more than a meditation on dancing, "Orchestra," his most famous work, offers the reader a meditation on desire. In "Orchestra," the conception of a universe ruled by the correspondences between microcosm and macrocosm, between the dance of the stars and earthly harmony, is but an instrument of persuasion in the hands of Antinous. His aim is to pierce the mystery of Penelope's desire, of that woman who rejects the offers of all her wooers in the name of an incomprehensible faithfulness to a husband who vanished twenty years earlier. Antinous launches into the lengthy harangue on dancing that makes up most of the poem precisely because he finds himself confronted with a refusal to dance that goes against his world view based on specular relationships. To his discourse filled with certainties, Penelope opposes another desire, which will not let itself be reduced to a relationship between the same and the same. It is thus the problematics of desire that connects Roethke's poetic sequence to its acknowledged subtext.

Another aspect of "Orchestra" was also bound to appeal to Roethke, for the poem's second stanza mentions Homer, whose mind "Became the wellspring of all poetry." Sir John Davies' text thus also places itself under the sign of filiation. In the fourth stanza of "Orchestra," Homer is said to have "forgotten" an episode in the story of Ulysses and Penelope: how the latter was wooed by the former. Therefore, Davies asks Terpsichore, the muse of light poetry and of dancing, to sing "a plain and easy melody" meant to fill the blank left by Homer in his own narrative. I will try to show while studying the fourth stanza of Roethke's "The Dance" that the existence of such a blank may very well be precisely what the act of writing revolves around in this poem.

Now for a few remarks concerning the general formal characteristics of the sequence.

This sequence marks a clear break in Roethke's poetic practice. He renounces the free verse that dominated in his former collections and reverts to a more formally aware type of writing. Each stanza ends in a period, interrogation or exclamation point; most lines are also end-stopped, and follow the structure of the syntax, and only a few enjambments subvert it, lines 7–8, 10–11, 15–16, 23–24, 37–38, thus essentially in the first two sections. Also, each section of this four-part sequence is itself made up of four stanzas in which a quatrain is followed by a dystich according to an *ababcc* rhyme scheme, a form about which Enid Hamer wrote that "its success is greatest in poems of a reflective or elegiac cast."[5] Most rhymes are accurate and only sometimes replaced by assonances. The same rhyme may also be found from one stanza to the next, or even from one section to the next, thus guaranteeing the continuity of the whole, despite Roethke's method of composition, which, at the time, was based on accumulation of single independent units. Finally, a strictly decasyllabic iambic pentameter predominates, with but few exceptions.[6]

Overall, it would be tempting to apply to this text a formula used by Dylan Thomas to characterize his own poetry: "a water-tight compartment of words."[7] For indeed, the impression we get after the initial reading is that of a locking of meaning within strict boundaries thanks to a formal set-up quite unprecedented in Roethke.[8] For such a variety of devices to be put to work here, we suspect that the stakes must be considerable, which the 1st section of the sequence will, I think, amply verify.

First Section: "The Dance"

The choice of the deictic "that"[9] that initiates the questioning establishes a relationship of interlocution between the subject of the statement *[énoncé]* and his reader, who will be addressed directly a little bit farther down ("O watch his body sway!") We are thus, from the start, referred to the other text where dancing was presented as a universal modality of motion as well as to the worldview expressed by this sometimes rather didactic poem, a view from which Roethke first seems to distance himself: the human mind was once inhabited by a dancing motion that has somewhat slowed down nowadays, and that is why it thought the universe capable of humming, that is, of producing music that regulated this inner dancing.

Yet the poet does not deny that the "great wheel" whose motion animated all things might be apt, "when it can," to set itself in motion again, and this seems indeed to be the case in this first stanza, in which the harmony of the spheres does somehow make itself heard, a harmony that consists in a "hum," that is, in a *wordless* song. While evoking that imaginary time when a womb-like universe used to regulate even the motions of the mind, a time of perfect correspondence between the whole and the one, ignorant of the symbolic cut, the stanza seems to reflect this imaginary order even in its phonic substance through the play on assonances and alliterations: thus "him," the pronoun which stands for "man," line 1, is echoed in "hum" at the end of line 2, which is a predicate of "universe." Thus, too, the nasal bilabial resonates in the alliteration: " . . . in the *m*ind of *m*an / That *m*ade . . . ," thereby creating an effect of imaginary continuity despite the break introduced by the change of line. Not to mention the internal rhyme *sing*-dan*cing* line 4, almost the whole stanza is saturated with line-to-line assonances which double the effect of the rhyme: slow*ing*-th*ink* (lines 1 and 2), m*ade*-gr*eat* (lines 2 and 3), wh*eel*-n*eed* (lines 3 and 4), pl*ace*-m*ade* (lines 4 and 5). Finally we observe a first chiasmus, perceptible to the eye if not to the ear through the typographical disposition of the signifiers "p*rom(*ise)" "*rom*p(ing)" directly one above the other, thus creating a symmetrical effect that confirms the imaginary anchoring of this passage.

The bears that make their appearance at the end of the first stanza are quite enigmatic. Perhaps Roethke felt some personal affinities with these animals, (as also with the elephants he mentions line 40) because of his own rather monumental stature and of his awkward gait? Stephen Spender, who refers to "the swaying elephantine dance of his huge body,"[10] further observes:

> In his poems, Roethke seems often to be dancing. This is not the dance transcended and purified in the poetry, the entry into a metaphysical pattern of theological joy of Auden or Eliot, nor is it the tragic dancing on the graves of the dead of Yeats—it is simply Roethke incredibly and almost against his will dancing. He is the boy who is waltzed round by his father of the whiskeyed breath; the sensual man swaying toward the woman swaying toward him; the dying man dancing his way out of his body toward God.
>
> There was never, one might say, such ungainly yet compulsive dancing, as in Roethke.[11]

But, in a less anecdotal way, the bears also function as what Michael Riffaterre calls textual interpretants.[12] Rather than

from his own mirror, Roethke borrowed these bears from Sir
John Davies' poem, where we read:

> Thus when at first Love had them marshallèd,
> As erst he did the shapeless mass of things,
> He taught them rounds and winding ways to tread,
> And about trees to cast themselves in rings;
> As *the two Bears,* whom the First Mover flings
> With a short turn about heaven's axletree,
> In a round dance for ever wheeling be.[13]

However, the disappearance of the capital B in Roethke's own
bears indicates that, altlhough he sets himself the task to "sing
and whistle romping with the *bears,*" Roethke does not simply
intend to repeat the specular dialectic on which "Orchestra" is
based, even though we may occasionally find other echoes of it
in the poem. By giving himself the bears as models, and not just
the constellations whose name they bear, (no pun intended),
the poet introduces a significant modification. Although in the
Elizabethan worldview, a specular and therefore imaginary relationship is asserted between the motions of the microcosm and
those of the macrocosm, it also seems that the constellations,
insofar as they are all named, insofar as their motion is regulated
and an object of scientific discourse, are already parlty involved
in a symbolic order.

This is not the case, however, with the bears whom the poet
undertakes to follow "Down a steep hillside" (line 8). Whether
they were seen under the benign appearance that they have in
children's books ("or was that in a book," line 9) or even behind
the bars of a cage, something of their radical difference remains:
for, contrary to men, they are completely involved in the real.

"A cáged | beár rárelly doés | the sáme | thíng twíce | In the
same way . . ." (lines. 10–11). Tight as the formal apparatus may
be with which this difference is approached, it still manages to
voice itself despite the vocalic chiasmus (*caged bear* . . . /
rarely . . . same) that seems to emprison it, also challenging the
iambic metrical framework that it modifies by introducing two
spondees.

With its natural swaying motion ("o watch his body sway"),
the bear's gait is pure rhythm, not subject to the rules of language. "This animal remembering to be gay" is the receptacle of
a "gay science" that cannot be taught, but that may reside in the
vital pulse that the poet would now like to find again, hoping for

a communion with the real that appears here in the shape of the inaccessible moon.

> I tried to fling my shadow at the moon,
> The while my blood leaped with a wordless song
>   (lines 13–14)

Gaining access to the real might precisely mean managing to dissociate the rhythm and the melody from the song[14], which would be tantamount to abolishing language or, at least, retaining only its vibration, separating the weighty alliteration from the signifiers that vehicle it the better to mime the bears' gait ("*To teach my toes to listen to my tongue*"), reaching the infra-linguistic confines where the space of *jouissance* opens up, which is also the space of pure animality.

But no master will be found to teach that dance ("Though dancing needs a master I had none," line 15), for this would presuppose possible transmission of a knowledge, and therefore symbolization that, on the other hand, can be avoided if the learning process is purely visual: "I saw," (line 7), "O watch," (line 11).

But so that the dance does not resemble the monotonous—since uniformly accelerated—motion of a falling stone ("the joyless motion of a stone," line 18) may one at least borrow the rhythm of other texts? This might be the meaning of line 19 of "The Dance" ("I take this cadence from a man named Yeats"), concerning which Roethke voiced a rather amusing denial: "But here's the Sir John Davies sequence, anyway. As you'll see, it goes back to the very plain style of the sixteenth century—Ralegh and Davies himself, really not Willie Yeats."[15] For what matters most here, is Roethke's determination to borrow a mere rhythm[16] from Yeats and, one might add, one of the phonemes that make up his name, the [ei] which permeates several signifiers in the stanza (*take, cadence, named, take, again, brain, came*) and several rhymes in the section as a whole (lines 11–12, 47–48, 53, 55–57, 91–93). Thus, subverting the practice of intertextuality, the only thing Roethke retains from an author is a cadence and a sound. But, besides the obvious element of provocation in this gesture ("I take it, and I give it back again"), one can see what it brings into play.

For in this quest for pure rhythm, we seem to be within the framework of what Julia Kristéva terms "a modality of significance in which the linguistic sign is not yet articulated as the absence of the object and as the distinction between the real and the symbolic," the locus of a "vocalic and gestual organization," that of the chora[17], the field of "semiotic rhythm: . . . indifferent to language, enigmatic and feminine, . . . a space underlying writing, . . . rhythmical, unchained, irreducible to its verbal, intelligible translation; . . . musical, anterior to judgment, but retained through one guarantee only—syntax."[18] In this first section of "Four for Sir John Davies," Roethke does indeed try to approach what Kristéva places under the category of the semiotic, "a kinetic, preverbal functionality, anterior to the positing of the sign," these "pre-œdipal semiotic functions of unloaded energies which connect and orient the body in relation to the mother."[19]

Whether the locutor is trying to reestablish a pre-œdipal relationship to the mother or an animal relationship to the real, unmediated by the symbolic, one can clearly see how melody and beat fit in here, since their indefinite succession refuses to crystallize itself into signifiers:

> For other tunes and other wanton beats
> Have tossed my heart and fiddled through my brain

It is the space of *jouissance* itself that is delineated here (together with the threat of collapsing into madness that the opening of this space entails, line 23); at its core is a void that can perhaps be found at the very center of the chiasmuses that are so frequent in this stanza: line 19—, [eik]/[kei] chiasmus in *take . . .ca*dence, slightly modified line 20—by substitution of the velar to the plosive—into *[eik]/[gei]* in *take/again*; finally the eye chiasm in *man nam*ed, line 19. It is also the same space that is created by the absence of a fifth foot line 23, as well as, perhaps by the absence of an ever-missing line in our text, namely the fifth line of the "rhyme royale" (*ababbcc*) used by Sir John Davies in his meditation and that Roethke, otherwise quite faithful to the form adopted by Sir John Davies in "Orchestra," precisely decided to omit. Allow me to quote Serge Leclaire here:

Any substitution or displacement of the letter could not even be conceived without the intervention of a "grain of object": should this ounce of real, small as it may be, come to lack, the letter is then reduced to an unequivocal system of signs and the line is fixed into a trace which says nothing about *jouissance*. For *jouissance* ... is the impalpable and irreductible reality of this lack, which is the very motor of the structural system.[20]

It seems to me that Roethke's text, at least in this first section, functions around this lack, this void; this may be why it is so fascinating to the reader; this may also explain why Roethke was so enthusiasic when he wrote it. Yet the text may petrify itself into discourse, as the fourth section of the poem will indicate.

A detailed study of sections 2 and 3 of the sequence, might reveal how the poetic subject tries to encounter the feminine other through the mediation of a third party, the ghost who makes several appearances throughout these middle sections. Relationship to the feminine other and acceptance of difference is nonetheless never guaranteed: one observes a constant tendency of the subject to lose himself in his "dancing partner" whose object he thus becomes. Only in certain lines do we find interplay between the subject and the feminine other, and this is always threatened by a return to polarization and reduction of the other to a specular image of the self, which is another way of negating difference. Further study of the two middle sections also reveals how the recurrent imaginary flesh-spirit dichotomy is but partly overcome, at times when the body of the subject becomes "the body of his fate," that is, a body inhabited by speech.

Last Stanza of Section Three

Resonance between body and speech is thus never viewed here as an absolute necessity: the "sensual cry" (line 67) that brings into play the voice, defined by Denis Vasse as that "link which structures man by opening him up to speech [and which] connects the chain of signifiers to the origin in the articulation of breath and speech, of blood and meaning, of man and woman,"[21] is now used paradoxically to introduce the "vision" that will allow Roethke first to integrate Dante's intertext in "The Vigil" and bring it into play, but then to further the process of imaginary fusion that was already at work in the preceding sections.

The shape that falls from heaven in the fourth stanza of "The Wraith" is probably what the title of the third section refers to.

In section 2, the intervention of the "lively dead" had been followed by a *music* (line 46) and had initiated a learning process; with the *vision* however, the mortiferous imaginary prevails again partly: the "shape" that is seen only reflects in its motion the dance of the lovers ("whirling slowly down," line 72); this shape appears "*impaled* on light," which reminds us of the way the couple "danced upon a *pin*" (line 58). Besides, as though by a phenomenon of reversal indicated by the anagram, the abolishing of sight ("and saw no more," line 70), *s-a-w*, is concomitant with the positing of a paradoxical essence ("w a s," *w-a-s*) that language fails to define and that seems to subvert the signifier itself as specularity manifests itself in its very substance. One should also notice how the signifier "impaled" fairly explicitly indicates the secret relationship between the light that accompanies the vision and death, which the end of the fourth section will confirm.

Fourth Section: "The Vigil"

The word "wraith" designates "the apparition of a person shortly before his/her death," that is, the hallucinated presence of a being at the very moment of its disappearance. The term thus fits in the paradoxical logic we have observed by combining being and nonbeing. We should also remember as we approach the section entitled "The Vigil," what it tells us of a body on the verge of dissolution, an almost dead body where speech is becoming extinct. And it is precisely for the dead that one formulates the prayers that, in English, are called "vigils."[22] It might thus very well be that this dead body, deserted by the Other's speech and by difference, appears at the center of what we are about to read.

I have already pointed out that the sequence as a whole is made up of four times four stanzas. Now, it so happens that here is yet another definition of the signifier "vigil" that seems appropriate here: "one or other of the four watches into which the Romans divided the night." (Shorter Oxford English Dictionary) "The Vigil" is thus the fourth quarter of Roethke's meditation, a redundancy hardly concealed by Roethke's use of two heterogeneous codes: that of the English language and that of mathematical numeration. The reiteration of the seme "fourth" in the full title of this section: "4. 'The Vigil'" echoes that of the numeral in the title of the sequence itself "*Four for* Sir John

Davies," and is followed in the first line of "The Vigil" by another mirror effect, which now affects the sound material itself. For line 73 opens with a quite spectacular consonantic chiasmus: *Dante attained*, which already seems to betray the poet's wish to offer his reader, earlier somewhat baffled by the reference to Yeats, the joy of an encounter free of surprises with this canonical text, an encounter revolving around the narcissistic pleasure of recognition. For Roethke begins the fourth section of the sequence with a direct reference to the author of *Purgatorio*, which he quotes line 74. Here is Dante's subtext:

[. . .] so, within a cloud of flowers which rose from the angels' hands and fell again within and without, a lady appeared to me, girt with olive over a white veil, clothed under a green mantle with the colour of the living flame. And my spirit, which now so long had not been overcome with awe, *trembling* in her presence, without having more knowledge by the eyes, through *hidden virtue* that came from her, felt old love's great power. As soon as the lofty virtue smote on my sight which already had pierced me before I was out of my boyhood, I turned to the left with the confidence of a little child that runs to his mother when he is afraid or in distress, to say to Virgil: Not a drop of blood is left in me that does not tremble[. . .][23]

By asking his reader the question "Did Beatrice deny what Dante saw" (line 76), Roethke clearly invites him to go back to his classics. However, a parallel reading of canto XXX of *Purgatorio* and of this first stanza of "The Vigil" makes it extremely difficult to interpret line 76. For in Dante's text, the vision to which the poet gains access is that of Beatrice herself, who must now lead him to Paradise where Virgil, who was until then his guide, may not follow him. The formulation of line 76 is thus quite disorienting, since in the text Roethke refers to, Beatrice is the very object of Dante's vision and the embodiment of hidden virtue. Beatrice can therefore but confirm "what Dante saw."

But perhaps we should see in the very form of this questioning a strategy aiming to circumvent what is being approached here. For the object of the vision is endowed with a frightening power: it is the power by which the subject's will is abolished ("a mighty power beyond his will") and thus represents another version of the woman mentioned in lines 28 and 29, where Roethke asked himself "Was I the servant of a sovereign wish?" It is also that, the intellectual contemplation of which presupposes a castration of the eye, since this virtue is *"hidden,"* hidden from the senses and since already in the preceding section, access to vi-

sion was accompanied by blindness. Does this vision yield access
to the *jouissance* of the mother, in which the subject would be
abolished? This is a possible interpretation, especially in the
light of what was observed concerning line 23 of "The Dance,"
but also in the light of canto XXX of *Purgatorio,* to which
Roethke was careful to refer his readers: here we just saw a
trembling Dante turning to the father figure who guided him so
far: Virgil to whom he said, at the beginning of *Inferno:* "you are
my master and my author" and whom he also designated in
canto XXX of *Purgatorio* as his "father." Now, at the gates of
paradise, Virgil is supposed to be relayed by Beatrice. With the
disappearance of Virgil, absent from Roethke's poem—although
an amputated trace of the name Vi(r)gil still remains in the
title—Virgil whose speech authorized Dante's in the same way
as Sir John Davies' speech authorized Roethke's, are we witnessing a dysfunctioning of symbolic castration?

The object of Roethke's vision is also that which language can
approach only obliquely. This, I believe, is the ultimate meaning
of line 76: "what Dante saw" is *and* is not Beatrice, for she,
after all, is nameable: it is something that the neutral relative
pronoun "what" but imperfectly describes, something that may
also reside in the silence introduced by the comma and dash at
the end of line 75, something that is located in the gap separating Beatrice from the virtue she is and is not, something that
may be related to what Jacques Lacan calls "the Thing," whose
characteristic is that it is "represented by something else."[24] It
is no wonder, then, that Roethke chose Dante's intertext here:
I quote Lacan's eighth *Seminar:*

> In this poetic field, the feminine object is emptied of its real sub-
> stance. That is what makes it then so easy to such and such meta-
> physical poet, to Dante for instance, to take a person who we know
> existed—i.e. Beatrice [. . .]—and to make her the equivalent of phi-
> losophy, even of sacred science, and to call on her in terms all the
> closer to the sensual that the said person is closer to the allegorical.
> One never talks so much in terms of love as when the person is
> turned into a symbolic function.
>
> We witness here the pure functioning of the place of what subli-
> mation tends towards: namely that what man demands, . . . is to be
> deprived of something real."[25]

As we can see, the intertextual strategy at work here is subtler
than may have appeared initially: it challenges the reader to put
his knowledge of the intertext to work within a problematics of

desire which the quoted texts support. I tend to think, however, that the speech of the Other ceases to be heard as soon as discourse takes over, which is the case as early as the distich with which the first stanza of "The Vigil" ends.

Whereas in "The Partner" the poet called himself "perplexed" (line 26) and the third section made room for the "incomprehensible" (line 49), he now takes refuge in aphorism, scanned by the "L" alliteration, both generalizing and relativizing the lovers' experience in a surprising gesture of denial of the vision that was just presented to us:

> All lovers live by longing, and endure:
> Summon a vision and declare it pure.

This fairly banal statement on desire seems to find its own confirmation in the mere recurrence of phonemes: [end] in *and endure* and [2 n] in summ*on* and visi*on*, but also attempts to nullify what line 76 might have suggested. Whereas line 76, taken in the context of the quatrain, allowed us to question the apparent tautology "Beatrice = What Dante saw," now, as if annexed by lines 77–78, the same line tends to signify that Beatrice could not have denied what Dante had seen simply because of the law that the distich claims to enunciate.

In the same way, lines 79–80 are characterized by their high degree of generality: "everything's astonishment." "Who leaps to heaven at a single bound?" echoes "This joy outleaps the dog" and reinstates the flesh/spirit dichotomy that had been temporarily suspended due to the intervention of the ghost in "The Partner" and "The Wraith." It is no wonder, then, if the links between the lovers become weaker now: "The links were soft between us," line 81. For it takes an intermediary link to unite the lovers, namely the Other's speech. And it is precisely this link that the poem is now going to try to do *without,* favoring a process of imaginary fusion between the subject of the poem and his "partner." By filling lines 81 and 82 with the "strange sounds" of the kisses exchanged through the [k . . . s] and [nd] pararhymes in:

> The lin*ks* were *s*oft between u*s*; *s*till we *k*issed;
> We u*nd*id *ch*aos to a *c*urious soun*d*

the poet reactivates the "dance" isotopy via the signifier "chaos,"[26] which, in Sir John Davies' poem, was presented as the antithesis of the dance. He thus situates himself within the frame of reference of the Elizabethan hypotext, where harmony is fully dependent on specular interplay between microcosm and macrocosm. It is no wonder, then, if synesthesia operates in line 83, creating imaginary confusion between perceptions: "The waves broke easy, cried to me in white"[27], while the *[w]* alliteration "*w*aves . . . *w*hite" seems to bring peace back to what was earlier described as "the ravaged shore" (line 68). In a similar way, the poem would like to present the partner as embodying the successful fusion of contraries ("She was morning in the dying light") resulting in negation of difference, but only manages to do so at the cost of a homophony (morning/mourning) made significant by the proximity of "dying" as well as by the title "The Vigil," whose polysemy I have already hinted at. Thus, the "death" isotopy asserts itself in this section, a fact to be connected with the growing uncertainty perceptible in a discourse now deserted by the Other.

While we read in line 63 that "The flesh can make the spirit visible," we now find out that "The visible obscures," a surprising example of double-talk as could already be noticed in lines 77 and 80, where doubt was suddenly being cast on the purity of the vision seen at the end of "The Wraith;" if a thing is as true as its contrary, a form of perversion of language sets in, following a mechanism in which, to use Denis Vasse's formula,

> one thing and its contrary are asserted about an object, which makes us into subjects of contrary utterances, tending to cancel the division, the splitting that constitutes us as speaking subjects, subject to speech. . . . When we claim to be saying, depending on the perspective, one thing and its contrary, we enter an imaginary, specular duplication where discourse functions by itself, disconnected from the speaking subject. . . . The appearance of a subject divided by speech constitutes, at the articulation of the imaginary and the real, the spring of the symbolic order. But if, in the imaginary effects of discourse, law remains ineffective, this means that, . . . the subject is not subject to Speech [parole]."[28]

These remarks seem fairly pertinent here, all the more so since I have tried to show how, in the preceding stanzas, the Other's speech was at work in a nonspecular intertextual dialectics, and how something was thus being articulated concerning the subject's relationship to his desire. It is not certain, however, whether this is the desire of the Other, as ruled by law, or, on the opposite, a transgression wish bearing on the side of the imaginary and of *jouissance.*

As a matter of fact, the third stanza of "The Vigil" presents the lovers caught in an ecstasy of the invisible that causes a *rupture* in the construction of the sentence while shedding ambiguity on the meaning of the preposition (does "with" complement "rapt" or does it have the same meaning as "together with"?) and also disrupting the iambic *order* that prevailed in the sequence with the introduction of a trochee and a spondee at the beginning of the line: "*Rápt,* we | *léaned fórth* | with *what* | we *could* | not *see.*" The lovers have given up playing "with light and dark" (line 66) and disjunction takes over, immobilizing positions into mutually exclusive alternatives without leaving difference any room for play: in this binary logic, night is "mocked" (line 89) and assimilated to chaos; yet the order which is opposed to it is not that of the law but of the imaginary.

Thus, synesthesia recurs in the syntagm "we danced to shining," shining being here substituted to the " lewd music" heard line 46, which came from a darkness now fallen silent.[29] Thus, also the metaphor of the dance of ideas that had introduced the sequence is repeated: a circular motion rules the progression of thoughts ("thought comes round again," line 87), as if the perfect correspondence between the motion of the stars and that of humans had been restored. The real once again becomes a network of specular relations where things capable of thought ("Things have their thought," line 86) are but so many reflections of a subject threatened with being scattered among all those fragmented images of himself: "they are the shards of me."[30]

This fragmentation is a prelude to the complete dissolution of the body that I think may be deciphered in the last stanza of the sequence. This stanza begins with a line ("The world is for the living. Who are they?") whose organization reproduces that of line 85 (a gnomic sentence followed by a question that makes unverifiable the law formerly enunciated) and that of line 41 ("The living all assemble! What's the cue?"). I would argue that in this line, the poet was attempting to unite all creation in a relationship to the real, mediated by his encounter with "the lively dead." It is now as if the subject had renounced the real as well as his own body that is abolished in the "form" of the partner: incapable of saying who the living are (line 91), the subject is equally incapable of determining whether he is one of them, which is hardly surprising, since being crossed out of the register of speech also means being crossed out from among those of the living whom only speech can articulate to the real and to the imaginary.

All that is left for Roethke to do is now to cast a retrospective glance on the three preceding sections by imposing on them the prism of a linear narrative progression, in order to secure for the entire sequence a univocal reading reducing it, for instance, to "the lovers' progress from obscurity to light." It is, however, difficult not to notice more regressive aspects that come to the fore here. What can we say about this element whose warmth and whiteness are so markedly opposed to obscurity through the [d] alliteration, contrasting with the softness of the semi-vowel that pervades the last two iambs of line 92 and almost all of line 93 ("She *was* the *wind* *when* *wind* *was* in my *way*")? Though he escaped this womb-like obscurity, doesn't the subject still dream of self-extinction in maternal jouissance ("I perished in her form")? Does his scattered body seek in the feminine other a shape that might contain him at last?[31] Or is he once more reduced to being the object of the other,[32] bathed in a feminized wind, dissociated from his own body, disembodied?

Let there be no mistake, in any case, as to the function of the intertext in these last lines. For if Roethke repeats literally in line 95 a formula used by Beatrice in *Purgatorio,*[33] the comparison here once again suggested with the itinerary of Dante, who also gains access to light in the conclusion of *Paradiso,* is a façade that conceals a fundamental difference: in canto XXX of *Purgatorio* Beatrice calls the poet by his name,[34] she acknowledges his inscription in the symbolic order, and therefore, despite Virgil's departure, the poet will be able to continue writing *Paradiso.* At the conclusion of "The Vigil," however, Roethke's use of the intertext cannot make us forget that collapsing into the imaginary is synonymous with mourning a body that is not articulated to the subject through speech: the flesh is relinquished by the spirit, the word, lacking a grasp on the real, leaps out of the world ("The word outleaps the world," line 96) in the same way as the joy of Ulysses' dog left behind the dying animal ("This joy outleaps the dog," line 44). And this is indeed the fall that, I think, is really described in the last two lines ("Who rise from flesh to spirit know the fall: / The word outleaps the world, and light is all.") For these lines cast a certain doubt as to the success of the enterprise that is coming to its end. On the one hand, those two maxims seem to utter a relative cliché, namely that spiritual elevation, once reached, allows man to realize how far he has fallen. But on the other hand, this somewhat unsatisfactory interpretation of the parataxis calls for a more literal one, namely that ascent from flesh to spirit results in a hidden fall into the imaginary. Then truly discourse, unmediated by speech that articulates it to the real, may well leap out: it still ends up, not in the radiance of Paradiso, but in the dull light of tautology.

Notes

The quotation in the title is from *The Collected Poems of Theodore Roethke.* (New York: Doubleday, 1975) 101–104.

1. Theodore Roethke, *On the Poet and his Craft: Selected prose of Theodore Roethke,* ed. Ralph J. Mills, Jr. (Seattle: University of Washington Press), 1966), 23–24.

2. T. S. Eliot, "Tradition and the Individual Talent." in: *Selected Prose of T.S. Eliot* ed. Frank Kermode. (New York: Farrar, Straus and Giroux, 1975), 38.

3. Theodore Roethke, *Straw For the Fire : From the Notebooks of Theodore Roethke.* ed. David Wagoner (Seattle: University of Washington Press, 1980), 209.

4. "«ego» always holds a position of transcendence vis-à-vis *you* ; nonetheless, neither term can be conceived without the other" ["«ego» a toujours une position de transcendance à l'égard de *tu* ; néanmoins, aucun des deux termes ne se conçoit sans l'autre."] E. Benvéniste, "De la subjectivité dans le langage" in: *Problèmes de linguistique générale, 1.* (Paris: Gallimard, 1966), 260.

5. E. Hamer, *The Meters of English Poetry.* (London: Methuen, 1930), 168.

6. In the notebooks of the years 1948–49, the following statement indicates the evolution of Roethke's poetics: "The decasyllabic line is fine for someone who wants to meditate—or maunder. Me, I need something to jump in: the spins and shifts, the songs, the rants and howls. The shorter line can still serve us: it did when English was young, and when we were children. (*Straw for the Fire,* 186)

7. Dylan Thomas in: *New Verse* 11 (Oct. 1934), 8.

8. The only equivalents can be found in *Open House,* Roethke's first published collection, in which the poet was precisely struggling with the question of atavism and literary heritage.

9. "This constant and necessary reference to the agency of speech constitutes the feature which unites to *I/you* a series of «indicators» belonging to different classes through their form and combinatory aptitudes.... First among these are demonstratives: this, etc." ["Cette référence constante et nécessaire à l'instance de discours constitue le trait qui unit à *je/tu* une série d'«indicateurs» relevant, par leur forme et leurs aptitudes combinatoires, de classes différentes.... Tels sont d'abord les démonstratifs : *ce,* etc."] E. Benvéniste. *Problèmes de linguistique générale, 1.* 253.

10. Stephen Spender, "The Objective Ego," in :*Theodore Roethke: Essays on the Poetry,* ed. Arnold Stein. (Seattle: University of Washington Press, 1965) 4.

11. Stephen Spender, *Objective,* 5.

12. This concept is used here following Michael Riffaterre's definition: "[textual interpretants] are mediating texts, either quoted in the poem or alluded

to: they themselves contain a model of the equivalences and transferrals from one code to another, and they lay down the rule of the poem's idiolect, guaranteeing, with the authority a normative grammar, a tradition, or a convention would have, the semiotic pratice peculiar to the poem." *Semiotics of Poetry*, (London: Methuen, 1978), 81.

13. Sir John Davies, "Orchestra." in: *Silver Poets of the Sixteenth Century*, ed. Gerald Bullett. (London: J.M. Dent & Sons LTD., 1947), 330. (emphasis mine).

14. The strategy at work in "The Dance" seems at odds with D. Vasse's own conception of rhythm: "if it is true that music, «incapable of expressing anything», as Stravinsky puts it, establishes «an order between man and time,» everything which denounces the confusion between the real and the imaginary allows us to live according to OUR RHYTHM within the speech that makes up man's body. Rhythm is duration made perceptible by the return of a point of reference and endowed with an original function of integration within time. Music, which is «incapable of expressing anything» makes us hear silence as the privileged locus of listening, of the return of speech. In the desiring suspense which marks it, silence is the trace of the subject about to be born.

Human time—that of the speaking subject—is subject to the rhythm of the repressed which returns. And what returns has been trying to utter itself since the origin: speech separates the subject about to to be born form its imaginary identifications." (Denis Vasse, *La chair envisagée*. (Paris: Seuil, 1988), 18.

15. From *Selected Letters of Theodore Roethke*, ed. Ralph J. Mills, Jr. (Seattle: University of Washington Press, 1968): To Peter Viereck, 21 June 1953, 191. In his essay entitled "How to Write Like Somebody Else," Roethke mentions this mystification as follows: "Oddly enough, the line «I take this cadence, etc.» is, in a sense, a fib. I had been reading deeply in Ralegh, and in Sir John Davies; and they, rather than Willie are the true ghosts in that piece." *On the Poet and his Craft*, 69.

16. And not a theme, as he did earlier with Sir John Davies. True, the last lines of Yeats's "Among School Children," also in iambic pentameters, do refer to dancing, but Yeats's Platonic meditation in the rest of the poem does not seem to have much in common with what Roethke is trying to come to terms with here:

> O body swayed to music, O brightening glance
> How can we tell the dancer from the dance?

The Collected Poems, of W.B. Yeats, ed. Richard J. Finneran. (New York: Macmillan Publishing Company, 1983), 217.

17. Julia Kristéva, *La révolution du langage poétique*. (Paris: Seuil, 1974), 25.

18. Ibid., 29.

19. Ibid., 26.

20. Serge Leclaire, *Démasquer le réel* (Paris: Seuil, 1971), 96. ["Toute substitution ou déplacement de lettre ne pourrait même pas se concevoir sans l'intervention d'un «grain d'objet»: que cette once de réel, si modeste soit-elle, vienne à faire défaut, et l'on voit la lettre se réduire à un système de signes sans équivoque et le trait se figer en une trace parfaitement muette quant à la jouissance. Car la jouissance . . . c'est l'insaisissable et irréductible réalité de ce manque, qui n'est rien de moins que le moteur du système structural."]

21. Denis Vasse, *La chair envisagée*, 16.
22. "Prayers said or sung at a nocturnal service, *spec.* for the dead." (*Shorter Oxford English Dictionary*)
23. Dante, *Purgatorio*. trans. John D. Sinclair (Oxford U.P., 1939) canto XXX, ll, 31–47 (italics mine).
24. Jacques Lacan, *L'ethique de la psychanalyse* (Paris: Seuil, 1986), 143.
25. Here is the full quote:

"Dans ce champ poétique, l'objet féminin est vidé de toute substance réelle. C'est cela qui rend si facile dans la suite à un tel poète métaphysique, à un Dante par exemple, de prendre une personne dont on sait qu'elle a bel et bien existé—à savoir la petite Béatrice qu'il avait énamourée quand elle avait neuf ans, et qui est restée au centre de sa chanson depuis la *Vita Nuova* jusqu'à la *Divine Comédie*—et de la faire équivaloir à la philosophie, voire au dernier terme à la science sacrée, et de lui lancer appel en des termes d'autant plus proches du sensuel que ladite personne est plus proche de l'allégorique. On ne parle jamais tant en termes d'amour les plus crus que quand la personne est transformée en une fonction symbolique.
    Nous voyons ici fonctionner à l'état pur le ressort de la place qu'occupe la visée tendancielle dans la sublimation, c'est à savoir que ce que demande l'homme, ce qu'il ne peut faire que demander, c'est d'être privé de quelque chose de réel. Cette place, tel d'entre vous, me parlant de ce que j'essaie de vous montrer dans Das Ding, l'appel-ait, d'une façon je trouve assez jolie, la vacuole." (ibid, 179.)

26. The concept of chaos is highly ambiguous in Roethke. Here, it is clearly opposed to dancing, as regulated by melody and music. Yet these are also conneced to chaos, as this quote from Roethke's notebooks indicates: "In the purely verbal medium if the condition of *music* is approached too closely, then tenuousness or (if the personality of the writer is strong) *chaos* ensues." (*Straw for the Fire*, 196. Emphasis mine) One can thus see how rhythm and melody may also point to a pre-linguistic stage—even anterior to the mirror stage in Kristéva's terms—and how they fully partake of the imaginary, since within the Elizabethan world view, they are connected with dancing which is conceived as a specular order superimposed on the real.
27. This cry, combining the whiteness of mother's milk with the whiteness of the shroud, is the last to be heard in the sequence.
28. Denis Vasse, *Un parmi d'autres* (Paris: Seuil, 1978), 42–3.
29. The problematics of "Orchestra" is echoed in this line proclaiming the triumph of light over darkness. See Sir John Davies' description of Penelope's palace: "[her palace] Shone with a thousand lamps which did exile/The shadows dark and turn'd the night to day." ("Orchestra," 8th stanza) The nature/artifice dichotomy, although not directly at work in Roethke's poem, partly reflects that opposing form and chaos.
30. In the logic of what I am trying to show, the breakdown of the name-of-the-father (in Lacan's terminology) is what brings about this "confusion between body and objects, . . . which always indicates the impossibility of gaining access to the game of identifications of the œdipal structure" (Denis Vasse, *Un parmi d'autres*, 122.)
31. "It is this limit which is constantly missing or inoperative among psychotics; hence they resort to an imaginary form which englobes them in hallucination" (ibid., 123.)
32. Concerning the fusion process at work here, Stephen Spender observed: "there inevitably is a stage when he becomes aware of the split between the «I» and «the other.»" Then it becomes a matter of life and death for him to

bridge the gulf between insideness and outsideness." (Stephen Spender, "Roethke: The Lost Son." *The New Republic,* 27 Aug. 1966.) A matter of life and death, indeed, except that fusion with the other, far from preventing it, makes the eclipse of the subject final.

33. *"When I had risen from flesh to spirit* and beauty and virtue had increased in me I was less dear to him and less welcome and he bent his steps in a way not true, following after false images of good which fulfil no promise; [. . .] he fell so low that all means for his salvation now came short except to show him the lost people; *for this I visited the threshold of the dead* and to him who has brought him up here my prayers were offered with tears." (*Purgatorio,* XXX, ll. 127–41)

34. "*Dante,* because Virgil leaves thee weep not, weep not yet, for thou must weep for another sword." (*Purgatorio,* XXX, ll. 55–7. Emphasis added.)

Works Cited

Benvéniste, E. "De la subjectivité dans le langage."*Problèmes de linguistique générale, 1.* Paris: Gallimard, 1966.

Dante, *Purgatorio.* trans. John D. Sinclair. Oxford: Oxford University Press, 1939.

Eliot, T. S. "Tradition and the Individual Talent." *Selected Prose of T.S. Eliot.* ed. Frank Kermode. New York: Farrar, Straus and Giroux, 1975.

Hamer, E. *The Meters of English Poetry.* London: Methuen, 1930.

Kristéva, Julia. *La révolution du langage poétique.* Paris: Seuil, 1974.

Lacan, Jacques. *L'ethique de la psychanalyse.* Paris: Seuil, 1986.

Leclaire, Serge. *Démasquer le réel.* Paris: Seuil, 1971.

Riffaterre, Michael. *Semiotics of Poetry.* London: Methuen, 1978.

Roethke, Theodore. *Selected Letters of Theodore Roethke,* ed. Ralph J. Mills, Jr. Seattle: University of Washington Press, 1968.

———. *Straw For the Fire: From the Notebooks of Theodore Roethke.* ed. David Wagoner. Seattle: University of Washington Press, 1980.

———. *The Collected Poems of Theodore Roethke.* New York: Doubleday, 1975.

———. *On the Poet and his Craft: Selected Prose of Theodore Roethke.* ed. Ralph J. Mills, Jr. Seattle: University of Washington Press, 1966.

Sir John Davies. "Orchestra." *Silver Poets of the Sixteenth Century.* ed. Gerald Bullett. London: J.M. Dent & Sons LTD., 1947.

Spender, Stephen. "The Objective Ego." *Theodore Roethke: Essays on the Poetry.* ed. Arnold Stein. Seattle: University of Washington Press, 1965.

———. "Roethke: The Lost Son." *The New Republic* 27 Aug. 1966.

Thomas, Dylan. *New Verse* 11 (Oct. 1934).

Vasse, Denis. *La chair envisagée.* Paris: Seuil, 1988.

———. *Un parmi d'autres.* Paris: Seuil, 1978.

Yeats, W. B. *The Collected Poems, of W. B. Yeats.* ed. Richard J. Finneran. New York: Macmillan Publishing Company, 1983.

The Author as Explicator in Wallace Stevens and Ezra Pound

MASSIMO BACIGALUPO

"I WISH . . . THAT HE WD. EXPLAIN HIS EXPLANATION"—EZRA POUND quoted Byron from memory towards the end of *Guide to Kulchur,* after a few particularly intense and fanciful pages called "The Promised Land." "That was in another country," he went on, "and a different connection, but I admit that the foregoing pp. are as obscure as anything in my poetry."[1] Actually, the country was the same, for the Dedication of *Don Juan* was written in Venice in 1818, and *Guide to Kulchur* in Rapallo 119 years later; and the connection was similar, for Byron was speaking of Coleridge's "explaining metaphysics to the nation," and Pound attempts in "The Promised Land" to explain (obscurely) his own metaphysics, and in fact goes on to put them in a nutshell: "I mean or imply that certain truth exists. Certain colours exist in nature though great painters have striven vainly. . . . Truth is not untrue'd by reason of our failing to fix it on paper."

Pound's is a naturalistic world, based on the assumption that there is something out there that it is the poet's business to communicate. But it is difficult to explain, and explanations of such truths will be difficult. So the approach to "The Promised Land" ends with a reflection on the means of expression, just as *The Cantos* end with a reflection on their own writing-block: "it coheres all right / even if my notes do not cohere" (Canto 116). This is really a more emotional repetition of the statement in *Kulchur*: "I mean or imply that certain truth exists. . . . Truth is not untrue'd by reason of our failing to fix it on paper."

It is a favorite pastime for critics to turn up examples of parallel statements in prose and verse by a given poet, which presumably cast light upon each other, or tell us something about the occasion of a poem. For example, M. H. Abrams quotes in the *Norton Anthology of English Literature* a John Keats letter of September 1819: "I never liked stubble fields so much as now—

107

Aye, better than the chilly green of the spring. Somehow a stubble plain looks warm." The quotation occurs in an introductory footnote for the ode "To Autumn":

> Where are the songs of spring? Ay, where are they?
> Think not of them, thou hast thy music too,—
> While barred clouds bloom the soft-dying day,
> And touch the stubble-plains with rosy hue . . .

The relationship between the two statements here is self-explanatory, though a consideration of the difference between the casual observation of the letter and the elevated music of the poetry opens up the entire question of Kėats's style, and a question of content. Can two statements say the same thing in such vastly different ways? Some would even say that the elevation in the verse is factitious, and that the naked perception of the stubble-fields in the letter is more spontaneous and more genuine. This really amounts to asking, What is poetry and why does one write it?

The young Wallace Stevens remarked that "It is a great pleasure to seize an impression and lock it up in words: you feel as if you had it safe forever."[2] He also said, famously, that "Poetry is a response to the daily necessity of getting the world right."[3] The latter (and later) statement concentrates on present satisfaction, leaving the sense of getting a job done only implicit. In fact, in a late poem Stevens appeared to deny the desire to preserve the moment:

> It was not important that they survive.
> What mattered was that they should bear
> Some lineament or character,
>
> Some affluence, if only half-perceived,
> In the poverty of their words,
> Of the planet of which they were part.[4]

While denying the importance of survival of the written word, Stevens still spoke of representation of events and phenomena (the planet), and representation implies survival. Here I would like to call attention to the surprising agreement of Stevens with Pound (in a common self-depreciatory mood) in pointing to the objective world and slighting the written word: "Truth is not untrue'd by reason of our failing to fix it on paper." Both are very much concerned with "getting the world right." A comparative reading of "The Planet on the Table" and Pound's final *Cantos* would be illuminating.

Stevens's poetry is often glossed with references to the essays in *The Necessary Angel* and to his letters, chiefly in connection with poetic theory, the subject of much of the poetry. A direct parallel between an impression and a poem, as in Keats, is possibly less easy to come by. Here however is an example. He writes on 3 October 1952 to Sister M. Bernetta Quinn:

> This morning I walked around in the park here for almost an hour before coming to the office and felt as blank as one of the ponds which in the weather at this time of year are motionless. But perhaps it was the blankness that made me enjoy it so much.[5]

On 12 November 1952 Stevens sent to *The Nation* a group of poems, among them *The Plain Sense of Things,* which describes the same scene as the letter:

> After the leaves have fallen, we return
> To a plain sense of things ...
>
> It is difficult even to choose the adjective
> For this blank cold, this sadness without cause....
>
> Yet the absence of the imagination had
> Itself to be imagined. The great pond,
> The plain sense of it, without reflections, leaves,
> Mud, water like dirty glass, expressing silence
>
> Of a sort, silence of a rat come out to see,
> The great pond and its waste of the lilies, all this
> Had to be imagined as an inevitable knowledge,
> Required, as a necessity requires.

The poem gives us more natural detail and a heavier theoretical apparatus than the letter, developing the theme of the consolations of philosophy, of the sovereign act of the imagination. The letter goes more quickly to the heart of the matter by speaking of the enjoyment of blankness. As for Keats, the relation between the two statements could be compared to that of a sketch to the finished painting. With several painters, for example Ingres, modern taste sometimes prefers the sketch to the solemnity of the final work.

Ezra Pound rarely, if ever, gave information on his walks and more mundane doings to his correspondents. His communications mostly relate to his reading, or comment on current events, sometimes bringing in anecdotes and references from memory. Still, since he wrote his letters and essays concurrently with his poetry, the former often function as a running commentary on the latter. Given Pound's insistence on concentration, the more expanded versions of the same statements are often to be found in the correspondence, rather than in the poetry. The sketch in this case is more expansive than the final painting. For example, in a letter to Clark Emery dated 16 October 1954, from St. Elizabeths Hospital in Washington, Pound writes:

> Incidentally John Ad/ to Rush in 1811 anticipates Gesell and is five years ahead of Jeff's approach from the other, or AN other angle.

> A decent Biddle (Alex) printed some "Old Family Letters" whether to avoid family suspicion I dunno, nothing on cover to indicate that they are Adams to Rush.[6]

Canto 94, written late September of the same year, begins impenetrably, yet memorably:

> "Brederode"
>   (to Rush, Ap 4. 1790)
> . . . treaties of commerce only,
>   Blue jay, my blue jay
> that she should take wing in the night . . .
>   Mr Adams saw thru the bank hoax . . .
> & the Medici failed from accepting too many deposits.
> Alex . . . , a respectable
>   or at least meritorius Biddle,
>   alive 1890
> "& consequently the corruption of history"
>   J.A. to Rush
>   18 'leven[7]

In the poem, Pound alternates quotation, inevitably opaque, with unambiguous generalization ("Adams saw thru the bank hoax"), but fails to make explicit the relation between Alexander Biddle and the quoted Adams-Rush letters, as he was to do some days later in the letter to Emery. He throws us into the deep waters of his fragmentary history, and as it were challenges us to sink or swim. But probably only an Adams expert could discover the source in the innocuously titled *Old Family Letters*. While denouncing "the corruption of history," and implying in his letter that the Adams-Rush exchange was too hot and had to be hidden away, Pound continues to hide it away. The champion of a conspiratorial interpretation of history, Pound couldn't but be himself a conspirator. This, by the way, is the point about the Dutch Brederode, mentioned by Adams in connection with the excessive reputation of Washington: "Brederode did more in the Dutch Revolution than William 1st Prince of Orange. Yet Brederode is forgotten and William [is called] the Savior, Deliverer and Founder."[8] Pound is saying rather cryptically that what Brederode is to Holland, Adams is to the United States—lost leaders, like Pound himself. It is also worth noting that the implicit negative reference to other Biddles (Nicholas of the Bank War, and probably US Attorney General Francis Biddle, who indicted Pound in 1943) passes unchanged from poetry to letter or viceversa: *The Cantos* are Pound's conversation, "the theatre, the record, of flux of consciousness."[9]

So far I have spoken of parallel statements, to be found in Keats as well as in Stevens and Pound, with possibly the interesting difference that in Pound the poetry is more condensed than the prose, in accordance with his poetics, while with the others the opposite is the case—the poetry develops a germ that is recorded more briefly in a letter. However, there is one kind of parallel statement where the process of expansion is comparable in Pound and Stevens, and that is the overt explication by the author of a given work or passage. Interestingly, we have a lot of authorial explications by Stevens, and very few by Pound. This is because Stevens's poetry has more of the character of the finished product, compact and self-contained, something that one can talk about and around, while with Pound the poem is not the well-shaped urn, but, as he often told us, a vortex, where it is difficult even to begin to ask questions, for everything leads to something else. Besides, while Stevens was very patient, at least as a letter-writer, with well-meaning enquirers and translators, and provided detailed glosses on some of his most famous and obscure poems, Pound was usually impatient, thinking of the next job and postponing revision and correction and clarification (which he occasionally mentioned) until it was too late. Here again, however, I would like to point out that Stevens also suggested several times that he was much more interested in what he was going to write than in what he had written. So both men were similarly concerned with making it new, rather than with dwelling on what was behind them.

Authorial explication seems to be a modern phenomenon. We only have to think of *Ulysses* with its tables and *The Waste Land* with its notes. But then one remembers Dante's letter to Cangrande, explaining the four levels of interpretation to be applied to the Commedia:

> ... istius operis non est simplex sensus, ymo dici potest polisemos, hoc est plurimum sensuum; nam primus sensus est qui habetur per litteram, alius est qui habetur per significata per litteram. Et primus dicitur litteralis, secundus vero allegoricus sive moralis sive anagogicus.[10]

Perhaps the similarity is not coincidental, for Joyce and Eliot were, like Pound, much concerned with the Middle Ages and Dante. But Stevens wasn't, except in his play on Ursula and the like. Still, he seems to have been naturally inclined to coded writing, and did use to a certain degree private symbolism, so that in some of his work he may well be the most obscure of modernists.

What status does authorial explication have? Stevens was quite willing to accept readers' responses as authoritative, and made frequent disclaimers about the value of his paraphrases. "What I intended," he wrote a correspondent in 1941, "is nothing." And went on:

> A critic would never be free to speak his own mind if it was permissable for the poet to say that he intended something else. A poet, or any writer, must be held to what he put down on the page. This does not mean that, if the critic happens to know the intention of the poet, it is not legitimate for him to make use of it, but it does mean that, if he does not happen to know, it is not of the slightest consequence that he should know, even if what he says the poem means is just the reverse of what the poet intended it to mean. The basis of criticism is the work, not the hidden intention of the writer.[11]

Stevens gets at the center of the issue with a lawyer's instinct, and he is right of course. Yet how many of us read through his 890-page *Letters* for clues to his poems, and are thankful, even at this late date, for a statement such as the following, about that perennial conundrum, "The Emperor of Ice-Cream":

> the true sense of Let be be the finale of seem is let being become the conclusion or denouement of appearing to be: in short, icecream is an absolute good. The poem is obviously not about icecream, but about being as distinguished from seeming to be.[12]

This is enlightening—up to a point. In fact, one may want to respond, with Byron (and Pound): "I wish he would explain his Explanations."

In this matter of authorial explication, I believe we have learned to take all the help we can get, that is, we do not disqualify a reading only because it is the writer's own, as we would have done in the days of the Intentional Fallacy. We know that no word will be the last, that all statements are provisional, may mean the opposite of what they say. But this radical doubt is just as pertinent to the statements within a text. For example, when Stevens in "The Plain Sense of Things" presents "this sadness without a cause," the bleakness of the fall weather in Hartford, as a victory of the imagination, is he just consoling himself by vindicating the pleasures of asceticism? The question is not irrelevant, for Stevens suggests as much when he says that his act of imagination is "an inevitable knowledge, / Required, as a necessity requires." One must survive, so one makes up a consolatory version of the event that one has to face. Stevens, we remember, had no patience with people who condemned escapism.[13] So I would say that our attitude to authorial explication has become wary but open, just as our present attitude to biographical interpretation. We have become less sure of what consitutes literature, where the well-shaped urn finishes and the fallacy begins. We have all been drawn into the Vortex.

As I have said, Pound had little patience, unlike Stevens, when questioned about his work, and was apt to throw out cryptic comments that have misled generations of critics. A famous instance is his remark about *Hugh Selwyn Mauberley* in a letter to Thomas E. Connolly: "The worst muddle they make is in failing to see that Mauberley buried E.P. in the first poem; gets rid of all his troublesome energies."[14] This has been understood, by Connolly and others, to mean that the character Mauberley is the speaker of the first poem, though the title unambiguously tells us that this is "E.P."'s (not Mauberley's) "Ode pour l'election de son sepulchre": "For three years, out of key with his time ..." Pound, who was puzzled by the monumentalization of the Eliotic *Mauberley* at the expense of *The Cantos* and *Homage to Sextus Propertius,* a marvelous poem, was only pointing out that the poem *Mauberley* buries (figuratively) "E.P." at the very start. The idea that Mauberley should be the speaker never even occurred to him. Once again, authorial interpretations are in themselves needful of interpretation. At best, they answer a problem with another problem.

So we do not have for Pound the long letters of self-enquiry in which Stevens tries to puzzle together an interpretation for the benefit of critic or translator. Though it is true that in writing to translators Pound did provide detailed suggestions, and a very interesting area of study would be the translation of *The Cantos* that he worked on in a sort of collaboration with his daughter. It may be that Pound rarely had correspondents who were curious and persistent and sensitive enough to conduct a discussion of his poetry. When in the 1950s Clark Emery was writing *Ideas in Action,* one of the first and still among the best studies of *The Cantos,* Pound went over his typescript with extreme care, even pointing out typos—and came up with such characteristic comments as the following: "why buggar up a good blue-jay, for example, by making it a SYMBOL of some bloody thing ELSE?".[15] Compare this with Stevens's "imagined pine, imagined jay,"[16] and the reference to blue jays in Canto 94, quoted above.

If Pound did not explain *The Cantos* at any length, he did occasionally give readings of them, especially in the St. Elizabeths years, when he would hold forth to his acolytes in the asylum visiting hours. One of his protegés at the time was a young painter, Sheri Martinelli, whose work Pound admired to the extent of having his Milan publisher, Vanni Scheiwiller, issue at his expense a booklet of reproductions of her paintings under the title *La Martinelli* (1956), with his own appreciative introduction. To Scheiwiller, who did not care for Martinelli's art, he justified it as explication of his own work: "There is more about my Cantos in ten of these reproductions than in all the prose comment yet written."[17] Pound was in fact conducting a sort of paternal love-affair with his pretty and strange young visitor, and the surprising reappearance of love as a dominant motif in the St. Elizabeths Cantos, especially the beautiful second part of *Rock-Drill,* is surely connected with this flirtation. It is not difficult to recognize Martinelli in the Sibylla and Ra-Set and Leucothea that are praised for their compassion and their bikinis in some moving and amusing passages: "Sibylla, / from under the rubble heap / m'elevasti / from the dulled edge beyond pain, / m'elevasti . . ."[18] Clearly, for the incarcerated poet, this late affection was an unexpected godsend, and he proceeded very thriftily to put it to poetic use.

After *Rock-Drill* was published in 1955, Pound read it at least once to his visitors, providing a running commentary, especially on foreign words that the young Americans could not be expected to know. Sheri Martinelli dutifully made notes in her copy of *Rock-Drill,* adding a few drawings of "Maestro." These notes have been preserved, and provide the only complete authorial commentary we have on a section of Cantos, though not everything is glossed. Sometimes a disturbance occurs, and the annotator gives up, as in this note for Canto 88 (dated 24 January 1958): "K . . . is here today. She's a fake. Cdn't make any damn notes because Grampa starts bellowin' & roarin' & showing off for the cunts who listen & DONT hear & who beam & dont love ought but self."[19] Sibling rivalry is common in interpretative communities (such as academia).

The notes are a commentary at second hand, as recorded by a faithful disciple, yet they fill in a good number of blanks, and allow us to see what Pound thought he was saying or wanted to suggest. For example, *Rock-Drill* is notorious for its deluge of Chinese characters, that (as we all know) are taken by Pound as ideograms, pictures of things. In the poem, however, he does not always say what he wants us to read in a given character. In the Martinelli notes we find that several of these come from the *I Ching,* a little-studied source for *The Cantos;* we also discover some improper innuendos. "Jen" (elsewhere glossed by Pound as man with erect penis) appears twice on the second page of the sequence.[20] But it is news to this reader that the character for heart "hsin" (Canto 87), is also phallic: "Grampa sez this 'is cock and balls but dictionary sez heart.' Grampa would." This throws quite a bit of light on the previous lines:

Mohamedans will remain———naturally———unconverted
If you remove houris from Paradise
      as to hsin

I suppose the Chinese sound *hsin* may also playfully echo our Western concept of sin. ("So much for sin!") The passage continues listing the kind of connections that Pound likes to posit tentatively:

In short, the cosmos continues
      and there is an observation somewhere in Morrison,
leading to Remy?
      Bombs fell, but not quite on Sant'Ambrogio.
Baccin said: I planted that
      tree, and *that* tree (ulivi)[21]

Since Morrison's dictionary is made up, as the *Companion to The Cantos* tells us, of "six quarto volumes," it would be hard to find the "observation" Pound is referring to even if we knew what it was about. The reference becomes a little less opaque with Martinelli's note: "Chinese dictionary on mind." The point seems to be, as in Rémy de Gourmont, the relation between intellect and sex. This is suggested by another gloss, apparently referring to the peasant Baccin's proud statement about the olive trees that he planted himself. The note says simply: "copulation's good effect." Whether Baccin's and Pound's amatory activity also kept the bombs away from their house in Sant'Ambrogio, Rapallo, or whether the RAF was trying unsuccessfully in 1944 and 1945 to stop the fun, the notes do not tell us.

There is plenty of this kind of material in the notes, often the product of afterthought, for Martinelli worked over the pages adding retrospective comments. For example, this is the opening of Canto 89:

> To know the histories
> > to know good from evil
> And know whom to trust.
> > > Ching Hao.
> Chi crescerà
> > (Paradiso)

Somebody familiar with Pound's system of quotations knows that "Chi crescerà" stands for a phrase in Dante's *Paradiso, "Ecco chi crescerà li nostri amori."*[22] The full phrase is translated in the margin by Martinelli, under Pound's instruction, as "Behold one who will increase our love" (though it should be "loves"). We may think we are moving in the sphere of heavenly love, but Martinelli's personal comment brings us down to earth with a bump: "Behold one who will increase our love—Grampa's excuse when he spots a weak-backed broad." This is to be taken with a grain of salt, for Pound enjoyed very little privacy at St. Elizabeths Hospital, but it does remind us of the perennial playfulness of *The Cantos*.[23]

Predictably, the notes are particularly rich in the amorous section of *Rock-Drill*. In a way, Pound was reading to Martinelli poetry that she herself had inspired. Here, of course, we can never be sure how far we can believe her notes, for she may be claiming for herself a greater role than she in fact had, or Pound in a flirtatious mood may have told her that she was meant in a given line, to humor her.

Canto 90 begins, as perhaps the majority of Cantos, with a quotation that has puzzled critics: "From the colour the nature / & by the nature the sign!" Martinelli, after writing at the beginning of this, the first St. Elizabeths love-Canto, "Sheri's Cantos," thereby as it were appropriating the sequence, notes that the quotation comes "from S.M.'s early letters." She herself wrote the words! On the other hand, the *Companion to* The Cantos tells us that the lines refer to the doctrine of signatures. I personally would favor the more intimate interpretation. The little muse herself speaks.

A few lines on, the fountain of poetry on Parnassus, near Delphi, makes a propitious appearance:

> Castalia is the name of that fount in the hill's fold,
>   the sea below,
>   narrow beach
> Templum aedificans, not yet marble
>   "Amphion!"
> And from the San Ku
>   to the room in Poitiers where one can stand
>   casting no shadow
> That is Sagetrieb,
>   that is tradition.

In reference to Castalia, Martinelli notes: "a vision dear Green Eyes had of her"—where Green Eyes is Pound, who may very well have told "her" that this was the import. Whatever we make of the note, it is worth pointing out that a "fount in the hill's fold" is in itself enough to suggest woman and sex. I have noted elsewhere that Pound was also thinking of Henry James's *The Sacred Fount,* of which he was one of the few admirers;[24] a Pound-Martinelli note refers us also to "Boethius, Consolations of Philosophy," where I have not so far found a fountain, but references to Orpheus (III 12), which may also be to the point.

The feminine image of the fold is then spliced by Pound with the masculine "Templum aedificans" that Martinelli herself later glossed as an explicit reference to phallic erection: "Templum aedificans, not yet marble". I quote from this later gloss (1960), which seeks to recapture the very moment of poetic origin that the critic is always pursuing:

> now let us begin..we are on the lawn of St. Liz.. under that great
> tree, an Elm, I believe..
>
> birds & squirrels are around us—
> two blue-egyptian blue posts are to our right..Merlin is sitting in a
> lawn chair..he wears a green sun-shade cap of crossed bands over
> his silvery gold copper hair..he is 1/2 naked..the sun causes him to
> become be-dew'd—it is wet and delicious..
>
> his mer-maid is sit-
> ting on a fawn-coloured coat "the deer skin"..at his left side..
>
> Merlin is of the opinion..that when he erects his love god..the
> crops will be good that year..
>
> his poem then..is in the act
> of erection..and rising..
>
> everything is rising..within it..[25]

If this is a dream, it integrates significantly the powerful dream
of Cantos 90–95, with its elaborate make-believe and its seren-
dipitous return to adolescent love-play. In the unlikely setting
of a D.C. Hospital for the criminally insane, Pound was once
again in touch with the deepest sources, personal and cultural,
of his poetry.

A final word about the heresy of authorial explication. We
know from Peter Brazeau about the time Elder Olson of the
University of Chicago, asked Stevens about Rouge-Fatima in
"Academic Discourse at Havana." After correcting Olson's pronunciation (it should be FAtima, not FaTIma), Stevens said "he
had originally intended to put in something like Helen of Troy
but decided the poor girl was overworked, especially in poetry,
and so he thought of another beautiful woman." Olson persisted:
"That's fine, but what about the rouge?" "Oh," said Stevens,
"that's just to dress her up a bit."[26]

If we turn to another lady, this time invented by Pound, Ra-
Set of Canto 91, we find a similar comment in the Martinelli
notes: "A name that came to him from the air." And a few
lines above:

> Miss Tudor moved them with galleons
> from deep eye, versus armada
> from the green deep
> he saw it,
> in the green deep of an eye:
> Crystal waves weaving together toward the gt/ healing

Pound is speaking of Queen Elizabeth's sea-green eyes moving
men and making history, as in the fight with the Spanish ar-

mada, and a literary source has in fact been found, for the image of the warrior-lover seeing shipwreck in the eye.[27] Martinelli notes dutifully that "Drake saw it in Queen Beth's eye." At this point she asked Pound the inevitable question: How did he know? "Grampa sez," she records, "I said so!" There is no answer but the text itself.

On 30 April 1993 John Ashbery visited my class in Genoa and read to my students a then-unpublished poem called "The Mandrill on the Turnpike":

> It's an art, knowing who to put with what,
> and then, while expectations drool, make off with the lodestar,
> wrapped in a calico handkerchief . . .

I pointed out that in Italian a "mandrill" is also somebody who is "lecherous as a monkey," and asked him if this was so also in English. He said: "That's very interesting, because *man-drill* would seem to have a sexual connection too, but I don't think the animal has that reputation in English." I then remarked that there was no further reference to the mandrill in the poem, and asked him what that peculiar animal was doing in the title. "Oh," answered Ashbery, "he's just there, on the turnpike."[28]

Notes

1. Ezra Pound, *Guide to Kulchur* (Norfolk, Ct.: New Directions, 1952), 295 (Ch. 52).

2. *Souvenirs and Prophecies: The Young Wallace Stevens,* ed. Holly Stevens (New York: Knopf, 1977), 48.

3. Wallace Stevens, *Opus Posthumous,* ed. Samuel French Morse (New York: Knopf, 1957), 176.

4. Wallace Stevens, "The Planet on the Table," *Collected Poems* (New York: Vintage, 1982), 532–33.

5. Wallace Stevens, *Letters,* ed. Holly Stevens (New York: Knopf, 1966), 762.

6. University of Miami Library. Reprinted by permission of University of Miami Library and Mary de Rachewiltz, agent for the Ezra Pound Literary Property Trust. Quotations from unpublished writings of Ezra Pound are copyright (©) 1994 by Ezra Pound Literary Property Trust.

7. Ezra Pound, *The Cantos* (New York: New Directions, 1995), 654–55.

8. Quoted in Carroll F. Terrell, *A Companion to* The Cantos *of Ezra Pound* (Berkeley and Los Angeles: University of California Press, 1984), 570.

9. Allen Ginsberg to Ezra Pound, ca. 1967, as reported by Michael Reck, "A Conversation between Ezra Pound and Allen Ginsberg," *Evergreen Review* 57 (June 1968). Quoted in J. P. Sullivan (ed.), *Ezra Pound: A Critical Anthology* (Harmondsworth: Penguin, 1970), 354.

10. *Le opere di Dante* (Firenze: Bemporad, 1921), 438.

11. Stevens, *Letters*, 390 (3 June 1941).

12. Ibid., 341 (1 June 1939).

13. See for example, Wallace Stevens, *The Necessary Angel* (New York: Knopf, 1951), 30. Compare comments on the Ivory Tower in *Letters*, 403.

14. Quoted in Thomas E. Connolly, "Further Notes on *Mauberley*" (a review of John J. Espey, Ezra Pound's *Mauberley*), *Accent* XVI 1 (Winter 1956), 59. The letter cited by Connolly is written in the persona of Dorothy Pound, and begins: "Dear Dr Connolly E.P. asks me to deal with your troubles as follows: The worst muddle . . ." The typing however seems to be Pound's. In the same letter, of which Professor Connolly kindly sent me a copy, Pound writes, with reference to line 3 of *Mauberley*'s "Envoi": "thou: book." Students of the critical history of the poem will be thankful for the tip.

15. Letter of 13 February 1953. University of Miami Library. Reprinted by permission of University of Miami Library and Mary de Rachewiltz, agent for the Ezra Pound Literary Property Trust.

16. "The Man with the Blue Guitar," final line (*Collected Poems*, 184).

17. Letter to Vanni Scheiwiller, 23 November 1955, quoted in Massimo Bacigalupo, "Ezra Pound e H.D. nel 1956–59: un romanzo epistolare tardomoderno," *Nuova Corrente* 106 (1990), 186.

18. Ezra Pound, Canto 90 (*Cantos*, 626). On the Pound-Martinelli relationship see H. D., *End to Torment: A Memoir of Ezra Pound* (New York: New Directions, 1979), and the Italian edition, *Fine al tormento* (Milan: Archinto, 1994), which includes Pound's own account of the affair. Martinelli (1918–1996) was also friendly with William Gaddis, Allen Ginsberg, Charles Bukowski, and Anatole Broyard (see Henry Louis Gates Jr., "White Like Me," *The New Yorker*, 17 June 1996, 69–70). Of Irish background, she took her name from her first husband, an Italian-American artist.

19. American Collection, Beinecke Rare Book and Manuscript Library, Yale University. Reprinted by permission of Yale University Library and the late Sheri Martinelli.

20. Ezra Pound, Canto 85, (*Cantos*, 564).

21. Ezra Pound, Canto 87, (*Cantos*, 593).

22. *Paradiso* IV, 105. Pound quotes this passage in Italian in "The Promised Land" chapter of *Guide to Kulchur*, discussed above.

23. According to a "visitor" quoted in E. Fuller Torrey, *The Roots of Treason: Ezra Pound and the Secret of St. Elizabeths* (New York: HBJ, 1984), 241, "A few of his closest disciples or helpers could come almost anytime, AM, PM or evening." This is unsubstantiated, and it would indeed be surprising that visitors should have been allowed without restrictions into a criminal institution. Torrey's spiteful book is largely a denunciation of Pound and of Winfred Overholser, the humane and influential director of St. Elizabeths Hospital, who are presented as conspiring together to fool the public with the fable of Pound's insanity.

24. Massimo Bacigalupo, *The Forméd Trace: The Later Poetry of Ezra Pound* (New York: Columbia University Press, 1980), 266. This study offers a detailed reading of the *Rock-Drill* and *Thrones* Cantos.

25. Sheri Martinelli, "The TAO of Canto 90 . . ." Stencil sent to Clark Emery with a letter postmarked 13 August 1960. University of Miami Library. Reprinted by permission of University of Miami Library and Sheri Martinelli. Emery commented wittily on his epistolar relation with Pound and Martinelli

in the poem "St. Elizabeths," *The Carrell: Journal of the Friends of the University of Miami Library* 21 (1983), 14–16.

26. Peter Brazeau, *Parts of a World: Wallace Stevens Remembered* (San Francisco: North Point Press, 1985), 210.

27. José-Maria de Hérédia's sonnet "Antoine et Cléopatre," as first pointed out by George Dekker in *Sailing After Knowledge*: The Cantos *of Ezra Pound* (London: Routledge, 1963), 105.

28. John Ashbery, "A Poetry Reading in Genoa," *RSA-Journal* 3 (1992), 29.

Charles Reznikoff: New World Poetics

Geneviève Cohen-Cheminet

LET US START WITH MARTIN BUBER'S STORY OF A HASIDIM LATER
Master called Abraham Yaakov of Sadagora.

Of Modern Inventions

"You can learn something from everything" the rabbi of Sadagora
once said to his Hasidim. "Everything can teach us something, and
not only everything God has created. What man has made has also
something to teach us."
"What can we learn from a train?," one Hasid asked dubiously.
"That because of one second one can miss everything."
"And from the telegraph?"
"That every word is counted and charged."
"And the telephone?"
"That what we say here is heard there."

Should one include in "everything man has made" other man-
made artifacts, then this parable may be consonant with some
of Reznikoff's concerns in his *Complete Poems* and *Testimony a
Recitative*: it stresses in dialogue form around a master-disciple
relationship, first that the world is a text waiting to be read and
interpreted, as interpretations precede understanding; second,
that within a framework of human-divine correspondences,
communication cannot be sundered from meaning and interpretation; and third, that one is charged for what one says or
doesn't say in an ethics of interpretive accountability.

However, this smooth conceptual framework seems at odds
with Reznikoff's poetic modernism and explorations. Ever since
Rimbaud wrote that "poetry says what it says literally and in
every sense," readability and availability of meaning have to be
addressed by any modern poet or reader.

In Reznikoff's case, my overall thesis is that despite an appearance of clarity, legibility, and accessibility, his poetry should be
read under the sign of an "obscure literality," or that obscurity

122

of meaning coexists with an obvious blinding readability. In his essay on *La littérature littérale* Roland Barthes expounded this idea of "une littérature du constat" *à la littéralité aveuglante* (*Essais Critiques* 69), an antipoetical literature if, by poetry, one means a singular discourse characterized by metaphor, analogy, symbols, and depth.

I argue here for an appraisal of the conflicting experiences the reader of Reznikoff's *The Complete Poems* and *Testimony* is confronted with: my contention is that Reznikoff explored the twofold possibility of a coincidence of communication and intelligibility in *The Complete Poems* and a distortion between communication and intelligibility in *Testimony*—one of the most arresting aspects of *Testimony* being this unwonted coexistence of clarity of meaning at close range and indeterminacy of meaning in a macro reading. Reznikoff's version of what Maurice Blanchot called *L'écriture du désastre.* I use Timothy Bahti's distinction here:

> Whereas "ambiguity" stood for a positive and valued attribute of richness in a literary text, "indeterminacy" bespeaks a limitation or failure of a text to fulfill its purpose, whether this be a literary work's purpose of expressing the truth about the human condition, or an interpreter's purpose of arresting the meaning of the literary work. (Graff 165)

Before launching into a more in-depth analysis of Reznikoff's limit-experiment in *Testimony,* I wish to probe first into the issue of a blinding clarity of surface meaning that may have misled critics into an invidious reading screen, stifling the reader's approach to Reznikoff. This critical belief includes two epistemological screens: Objectivism, the intentionalist screen; and political commitment, the contextualist screen.

"A Blinding Readability": The Critical Belief

Reznikoff is routinely pigeonholed as an objectivist poet[1] intent on showing "particulars" as they are, excising the self from his poems, thus achieving and relishing the semantic matrimony of the signifier and the signified.

The Objectivist Screen

An oft-quoted passage is commonly interpreted as Reznikoff's positing the possibility of an adequacy between the writer's intentions and the language he uses.

I had been bothered by a secret weariness
with meter and regular stanzas
grown a little stale. . . .
I saw that I could use the expensive machinery
that had cost me four years of hard work at law
and which I had thought useless for my writing:
prying sentences open to look at the exact meaning:
weighing words to choose only those that had meat for my
    purpose
and throwing the rest away as empty shells.
I too could scrutinize every word and phrase
as in a document or the opinion of a judge
and listen, as well, for tones and overtones,
leaving only the pithy, the necessary, the clear and plain.
            Complete Poems II: 172

My contention is that, within the context of his *Early History of a Writer*, "the pithy, the necessary, the clear and plain" rather point to Reznikoff's awareness of the contingency of the symbolist and Romantic literary canon.[2] His radical departure from past verse practices[3] may have been chronologically misread as Reznikoff's enduring trust in an overlapping of the sign with the signified.

My second contention is that law school may have misled a seventeen-year-old Reznikoff into thinking there could ever be such a thing as "plain language," what Stanley Fish called, "the rule of law—of perfectly explicit and impersonal utterances—" (*Doing* 5),

The law that we studied
was not always the actual law
of judges and statutes
but an ideal
I found it delightful
to climb those green heights,
to bathe in the clear waters of reason,
to use words for their daylight meaning
and not as prisms
playing with the rainbows of connotations.
            Complete Poems II: 168

that could never trap a mature writer looking back on his formative years. Now, why could objectivism claim to posit an overlapping between signifying intention and language? Because of the assumption that the poet's self and emotions were not to interfere in perceptions and language. Reznikoff often expounded this idea, relating law and literature to objectivism:

> With respect to the treatment of subject matter in verse and the use of the term "objectivist" and "objectivism," let me again refer to the rules with respect to testimony in a court of law. Evidence to be admissible in a trial cannot state conclusions of fact: it must state the facts themselves. For example, a witness in an action for negligence cannot say: the man injured was negligent in crossing the street. He must limit himself to a description of how the man crossed: did he stop before crossing? Did he look? Did he listen? The conclusions of fact are for the jury and let us add, in our case, for the reader.
>
> [Let] me add to this the following . . .: "Poetry presents the thing in order to convey the feeling. It should be precise about the thing and reticent about the feeling . . .," "A rigour in seeking the objective correlative of emotion is a strong point of most Chinese poetry of all periods." (The phrase "the objective correlative," as you know is Eliot's)(*First, there is the Need* 8)

Of course, Reznikoff opted for conciseness and linguistic fasting, he was linguistically abstemious:

> Let me begin with some lines which illustrate, in a way, my platform—if I may use a political expression—as a writer of verse.

>> Salmon and red wine
>> and a cake fat with raisins and nuts:
>> no diet for a writer of verse
>> who must learn to fast
>> and drink water by measure.

>> Those of us without house and ground
>> who leave tomorrow
>> must keep our baggage light:
>> a psalm, perhaps a dialogue—
>> brief as Lamech's song in *Genesis,*
>> even Job among his friends—
>> but no more.
>>
>> San Diego Archives; *Complete Poems* II: 76

But he eschewed his status of author, lord of the signs and master of the signifying, bearer of explicit intentions. One might hear Wimsatt and Beardsley's criticism of intentional fallacy in this 1969 poem.

Whenever my sister used to practice
a certain piece on the piano
and came to a certain part—
not particularly good she thought—
a bird would fly to the windowsill
and sing along for a few notes.

The bird must have heard
what the player,
and perhaps the composer himself,
did not hear; and I am reminded of a Hindu saying:
a work of art has many faces.

Complete Poems II: 91

A "forgetfulness of self" (Reznikoff), a wish to efface the poet's presence, is congruent with the idea that a work of art has an autonomous unexpected life, pragmatically independent from the writer or the critic, who have little mastery over the explicating process. Interpretation is translated into the metaphor of dialogue between the piece of music and the bird's song: in Gadamer's terms, the reader brings to a text a pre-understanding constituted by his own horizon (bird's tune), is an "I " addressing the text as a "Thou" (piano piece), so that this text is an event produced by the fusion of two horizons. Reznikoff was therefore sensitive to "the unavailability of literal meaning" (Fish 4), meaning and interpretation being reader-relative.

To forestall any misconception of this "forgetfulness of self," it should be noted that a refusal of "A Song of Myself" does not entail any losing of the observer into the observed. Reznikoff draws the line between the poet and the world, by underscoring the impossibility of empathy with the object:

A tree in the courtyard blossomed early this spring
with large purple and white flowers
but the weather turning cold
and a cold wind blowing day after day
many of the petals have fallen
and the rest are withered and streaked with brown.

The warm sun is shining again
and a bird chirping away in the branches;
but what is its song?
A prayer for the dead flowers?

Complete Poems II: 209

There are two noteworthy features: the two unanswerable questions and the oppositional matrix of the poem positing "but" as a principle in perception. To search for intentionality outside the human realm into the nonhuman, that is, nonlinguistic realm is a temptation. But ultimately there is no answer, an aporia subsists, and only interpretations remain.

To construe the meaning of Reznikoff's work within an intentionalist (objectivist) approach seems inconsistent with Reznikoff's own mature awareness of the instability of reader-relative meanings.

The Contextualist Screen

A second well-grounded approach to his work is contextual. Context, historical or politically-oriented, becomes an instrument for determining the relevant meaning of his poems. The overriding concept of political commitment works as an epistemological screen. Richard Gray thus defined Reznikoff's "urban imagism":

> a poetry that alerts us to the loneliness, the small ironies and amusements, and the numbness of the immigrant in the urban tenement. In the best of his earlier, shorter poems Reznikoff refuses to moralize, to withdraw from the experience in order to comment on it or "place" it; the lives of the poor in the city possess an integrity that he chooses simply to respect and record. . . . (Gray 66)

The poet is shrunk to an objective photographer reporter of the real holding up a mirror to nature, and Gray came full circle when he added: " . . .—the social comment is all the more powerful for remaining implicit: the politics issues directly out of the urgency, the intensity with which the poet attends to the scene." (Gray 67).

To respect, to record, to attend to the scene are potent words highly irritating to anyone attentive to what Reznikoff wrote on the deceptive nature of interpretation. He repeatedly stressed the dangers of an essentialist transitivity between the literary and its extra-linguistic referential. Reznikoff maintained an ethical intransitivity between the two, through the channel of ethics, though not that of aesthetic formalism.[4]

I will suggest two examples. First, through the channel of political ethics, Reznikoff expressed a diffidence towards the confusion between literature and history:

> Reading some of the German poets of the last century;
> sad, yes, but sweet and gentle.
> Just then a knock on the door
> and I opened it:
> Hitler!
>
> *Complete Poems* II: 207

This poem starts in medias res with "reading," as if there were no threshold between the poem and common speech or action and establishes a nonmediated relationship between the reader in the poem and the reader of the poem. The segment "sad, yes" is enough to set up an imaginary dialogue between the enlightened amateur and the arch-reader. This immediacy conveys intimacy congruent with the closed room. The knock on the door tears away unity, but the door concretises the room in retrospect. The choice of the unexpected visitor needn't be elaborated upon. Suffice it to say that poetry reading can lead to misreading politics.

This poem indicts the reading practice that, through the theory of reflection, induces readers to believe literature is a duplicate of the real. Of course, Reznikoff's stance is contingent in Rorty's sense, but its historicity is on the enunciative and pragmatic side, not in any essentialist relation to the referential world.

Second, through the channel of literary ethics, Reznikoff expressed a diffidence towards the realist fallacy. Reality is valuated, axiologically oriented by the viewer's literary or academic ready-made reading grids:

> Young men and women in a ballet
> on the platform:
> how romantic!
> And a young man is climbing a shaky ladder
> to photograph it:
> this is realism.
>
> *Complete Poems* II: 210

Such categories as realism or romanticism contaminate perception to the point that the theatricality of any literary perception is overlooked. The ballet is misread into love or real life. In Habermas's words, signification, on the side of fiction, is read as a proof of validity (pretension to truth in real-life communications) (262–63).

This is our leading thread into Reznikoff's conception of perception as discontinuous.

Walking in New York

Fifth Avenue has many visitors
and many of these have cameras:
they take pictures of themselves, of course,
or of buildings,
and even of trees in Central Park.

But I have yet to see anyone
taking a photograph of the old woman
who stands on the sidewalk
wearing the blanket in which she has slept on a bench:
her stockings fallen
and showing her naked legs
streaked with black dirt
her grey hair dishevelled
and her face also streaked with smudges.

II

The tramp with torn shoes
and clothing dirty and wrinkled—
dirty hands and face—
takes a comb out of his pocket
and carefully combs his hair.

Complete Poems II: 208

Reznikoff captured disconnected images of fallen femininity and male fastidiousness. Discontinuity as a metaphor is acted out in the break between the poems and the dashes within the second poem. A paratactic style goes hand in glove with this phenomenological approach. Nowhere is to be found the age-old antinomy between photographic and literary representations. Reznikoff took issue with the need to duplicate the world in its selfhood and the need of self-representation. Precoded images blind to destitution and miss truth because reality is not equatable with realism, literary or photographic. There is, in that respect, a strong analogy between Reznikoff and George Perec's *Approches de quoi?* in which Perec called not for an exotic anthropology but for *une anthropologie endotique* (endos = within).[5]

So that the poetical real is the linguistic product of a conscience selecting, constituting, interpreting rather than mirroring the world. Perception inheres more in consciousness and intellect than in eyesight. Poetry is intentional in Husserl's and Ingarden's sense of an intentional act, object-oriented within a *lebenswelt,* a lived world.

Construer of the World

Departing from these critical ruts has enabled us to see hermeneutics as Reznikoff's mode of "being-in-the-world."[6] Reznikoff is less a recorder than a construer of the world, using poetry as a displaced hermeneutical discourse on reality, tentatively setting interpretive constraints and obliquely providing the reader with alternative interpretations or questions. Examples abound from:

> Graffito:
> Do not underestimate the value of an education;
> how else could one scribble
> this on a wall?
> *Complete Poems* II: 98

which may prove a tribute to educators; to three clouds over Central Park:

> Three clouds—
> steps
> leading into the blue sky:
> is this part of the ladder
> Jacob saw
> when he slept in the wilderness?
> But, unless my eyesight is failing,
> there are no angels, ascending and descending,
> upon it now.
> *Complete Poems* II:103

which graft a biblical interrogation about the absence of God on perception; to a banal crossroads:

> Sometimes, as I cross a street
> and automobiles come speeding towards me.
> But of course, I am much better off
> than the traveler in a forest—long ago—
> whom a pack of wolves pursue.
> *Complete Poems* II: 210

which grafts spatial perceptions on memory, using again a contrastive pattern. And finally, even past and present collide in a Greek linguistic heritage:

> The victorious Greeks before Troy, according to Homer,
> spoke "winged words" and Achilles
> was "swift of foot."
> Why then should we in New York
> reproach ourselves
> about our hurry?
>
> *Complete Poems* II: 101–2

This is usually belittled as humor. I choose to read in those poems the cognitive weight poetry has, less in terms of what one can learn thematically from poetry but more in what the poem, "itself an object of experience" (Gelpi 421), metalinguistically reveals about the issues of language, meaning, and interpretation.

These issues cover ground common to law and literature and underlie our last part.

Testimony: A Limit-Experiment

Indeed, if there is no such thing as literal meaning, if meaning is reader-relative, if only interpretations remain, the question of "constraints [set] on interpretive desires" (Fish 6) is invested with ideological relevance in law and literature.

Language? Reznikoff may have hoped for an overt "daylight meaning" but he posited that meaning was reader-relative.

Meaning? If relativism precludes literal meaning, or "once words have been dislodged as the repository of meaning" (Fish 7), then only interpretations are left.

Interpretation? If meaning is something the interpreter constructs, the possibility of objectivity in interpretation is null and void.

Question: How do literature and the law set constraints on interpretations? Is an ethical intransitivity enough to set an interpretive limit? Or seen from another angle: what becomes of a fact when the witnessing conscience that experienced it, that intended it, has disappeared and when only a linguistic testimony of this experience remains? Those testimonies are per se linguistic, language shouldering the problem of "how to translate knowing [and experiencing] into telling" (*The Content of the Form* 1).[7] This entails that any human experience, because of its linguistic testimony, is, by the nature of language, subjected to the question of its reality, truth value, legibility, and interpretation.

This is where the issue of "blinding readability" steps in. In *Testimony,* Reznikoff-the-construer-of-the-world holds back interpretation and foregrounds facts. *Testimony* evidences an illusive, destabilized micro-readability while macro-readability is held in abeyance. To paraphrase De Man, the reader confronts a limit-experience of "blindness and insight" at the same time. I shall of necessity confine myself to three points.

Testimony a Recitative

This is a 528-page-long collage of fragment poems, whose subject-matter was taken from thousands of law cases culled by Reznikoff in judicial archives in various libraries.

The general structure is loose, along temporal and spatial lines:

volume 1:   1885–1890: the South, the North, the West
            1891–1900: the South, the North

volume 2:   1901–1910: the South, the North, the West
            1911–1915: the North, the South, the West

Two paratextual notations, the incipit line and the epigraph, establish the reading contract. The incipit stresses the dual notions of authenticity and fictionality:

Note: All that follows is based on law reports of the several states. The names of all persons are fictitious and those of villages and towns have been changed. C.R.

and the detached New Testament epigraph advises against judgmental reader-responses, "Undisciplined squads of emotion." (Eliot, *East Coker*)[8]

Let all bitterness, and wrath, and anger, and clamour and railing, be put away from you, with all malice. (Ephesians, IV, 31)[9]

This paratextual contract thus serves as a reading contract but also as a metatext, a literary assessment of Reznikoff's discursive activity.

The first salient aspect is the generic transformation of the poems, which destabilizes the reader's expectations, and the second aspect is the overall nonnarrativity that counters any attempt to reduce the book to a neat metaphysical and humanistic message.

A Hybrid Fragment (Hypertext)

My line of approach is that *Testimony a Recitative* is not "a mimetic imitation," a prose document just versified into a poem,[10] but a hybrid fragment, a metanarrative, *un palimpseste,* in Gerard Genette's definition: "un texte au second degré, texte dérivé d'un autre texte pré-existant" (*Palimpsestes* 13). After Genette, we will call the judicial source document a hypotext, and Reznikoff's poem a hypertext.[11] A "hypertextual reception" approach (436) will guide our reading towards the transformative procedures informing the relation between the hypo- and hypertexts.

And the result of this transformation is neither a judicial testimony nor a standard poem, but a hybrid hypertext, a hybrid collage of fragments, called *a Recitative,* which retains none of the traits with which a reader normally associates a testimony as a genre ("horizon of expectations").

Throughout *Testimony,* Reznikoff systematically omitted dates and places of events within a loose geographical frame that is of little relevance. See:

The South-Machine Age
4
Betty was about eleven. She had no regular work at the mill
but did one thing and then another
and sometimes would take shirts to a table
attached to a mangle.

That morning the machine had not been started
and when she had placed the shirts on the table
[she] rested her fingers on the rollers;
and another little girl who also worked in the mill
started the machine:
it caught Betty's arm and crushed it.

Testimony II: 91

A side point here: as may be inferred from what was said earlier, no unique sociological interpretation through context will be

considered apposite to account for this blindingly simple poem.
Although most critics hold that *Testimony* is an indictment of
industrial destructiveness, set in the days when America was
changing from an agrarian republic to an industrial superpower
(Shevelow 293, Franciosi 177), I contend that this contextualist
approach is disqualified by Reznikoff's distrust of social realism,
and does not do interpretive justice to too many such poems as:

The South-III-Children

1

Jessie was eleven years old, though some said fourteen,
and had the care of a child
just beginning to walk—
and suddenly
pulled off the child's diaper
and sat the child in some hot ashes
where they had been cooking ash cakes;
the child screamed
and she smacked it on the jaw.

Testimony I: 127

or,

The North-Streetcars And Railroads

9

The first thing he knew the light of the train's engine was on him
and it was "zip"—
and all over.

Testimony II: 143

The hypertextual approach, by contrast, alerts the critic to
the gap between the normative features of a judicial testimony
(hypotext) and the choices informing Reznikoff's strategies in
the hypertexts. Specifics of time and place are irrelevant and
crimes or violence demotivated. Even the ultimate sentence is
left out: the reader takes stock of a death never accounted for.[12]

13

The murderer walked through the woods towards his victim
along logging paths no longer used:
rubbers on his feet to keep the mud from his shoes
and holding an umbrella in case it rained.

Testimony II:206

Further, Reznikoff removed or changed names[13] that are the legal markers for legal authentication. There remains a testimony without witness, and a narrative gap that Reznikoff filled by distinctly introducing *his* voice as *the* narrative voice. Reznikoff asserted his narrative point of view by depriving witnesses of narrative authority over their own testimonies. The original witness/narrator becomes narrated, and may seem to be dispossessed of his/her discourse, but the advantages of such a narrative strategy are as follows: Reznikoff neutralized the ambiguous status of a guilty/innocent witness inherent in any testimony.[14] He did not rewrite the facts in the light of the verdict, or of any hypothetical truth that the trial might have reached, in an inverted narration that would go from verdict to testimonies. Most poems have a narrative inertia, suspended before the verdict.

This generic manipulation destabilizes our expectations, in a microreading. Communication and intelligibility do not coincide, and the reader is left with a hybrid hypertext fraught with unanswered questions.[15] Is Justice as institution useless to redress wrongs, only an objective ally of the powerful, and occasionally a means of vindicating people's rights? Is it dissociated from the concept of a transcendent justice? Is guilt universal, the north no better or worse than the south or west, and ethnic identity no warrant of moral conduct? Has this nation been built on an impossible retributive justice? *Testimony* as crime without punishment; or more Biblically, has America been founded on serialized crime and the never-enacted punishment of the murder of Abel by Cain?

In my view, the key impact of this hypertextual manipulation is to force attention away from message to form. *Testimony* is a rhetorically determined act.

The Issue of Non-narrativity

The second means used by Reznikoff to hold back interpretation is his programmatic use of nonnarrativity in a macro-reading. Reznikoff used only nonnarrativity in *Holocaust* and *Testimony*. He used the narrative form in *The Lionhearted, A Story About The Jews in Medieval England* (1944), a novel based on the history of the Jews of York in the twelfth century, and in *The Jews of Charleston, A History of an American Jewish Community* (1950):

> This history was undertaken, as part of a bicentennial celebration
> in the autumn of 1950 of the continuous existence of Charleston's
> Jewish community, in the belief that there should be a history of the
> community from the beginning to the present—a history showing of
> necessity, if fully told, how the community was and is integrated
> in the larger community of the city . . . , one of the oldest Jewish
> communities in the country. (*Foreword,* ix)

> History, as such, is of little value to most of us except as a guide
> in the present. . . . It is the purpose of this history to show how the
> Jews of Charleston became Americans of their region, and remained
> Jews. (x)

If, as Hayden White convincingly demonstrated on the Annals
of Saint Gall, the form has content, if narrativity "entails ontological and epistemic choices with distinct ideological and even
specifically political implications" (*The Content of the Form* IX),
and a traditional narrative reveals an author's "conceptions of
historical reality" (5), then Reznikoff's commitment to the narrative in the *Lionhearted* and *the Jews of Charleston* is consonant with a specific representation of temporality, with the idea
of fundamental continuity in Jewish life: events are "revealed
as possessing a structure, an order of meaning" (5) and gaps
in the fabric of the narrative never threaten the Jewish "order
of meaning."

However, despite critics' claims, I find the internal narrative
mode of the poems is at odds with the general nonnarrative form
of the book. To appreciate this, see how Reznikoff deliberately
avoided the features of traditional narrativity.

There are no well-marked beginning, middle and end phases
in the corpus of poems, "no order of chronology," "no order of
meaning" (White).

There is no plot "if by plot we mean a structure of relationships by which the events contained in the account are endowed
with a meaning by being identified as parts of an integrated
whole."(*The Content of the Form* 9)

There are no diacritical markers for ranking the importance
of events: Reznikoff occasionally added titles to subparts but on
the whole, random discontinuity governs the articulation of the
discourse. Poems are juxtaposed,[16] but juxtaposition doesn't
necessarily make sense.

As for narrative closure, that summing up of the 'meaning' of
the chain of events" (16), as for a teleology of history, the reader
is frustrated again. White aptly phrased this: Reznikoff "does not

so much conclude as simply terminate."(5) *Testimony* could be prolonged and could have been stopped at any other time. Time is paratactic and narrative reactivation of judicial hypotexts is possible ad infinitum. *Testimony* is a *discours infini* (Blanchot).[17]

This is all the more significant as, again, "[t]he demand for closure is a demand, as [Hayden White] suggests, for moral meaning, a demand that sequences of real events be assessed as to their significance as elements of a moral drama." (21).

If White's intuition is to be trusted, if "narrativizing discourse serves the purpose of moralizing judgements" (24), of "[representing] the moral under the aspect of the aesthetic" (25), then what is the moral of nonnarrativity in *Testimony*?

To me, all these clues, the lack of a plot and chronology, the denial of a teleology, the preclusion of a meaningful resolution, belie any attempt on the reader's part to reduce *Testimony* to a metaphysically[18] clear message of humanism.

To the question: why did Reznikoff then launch into 528 pages of horrendous violence, I suggest one answer might be found in Judaism.

"If Not Now, When? If Not Me, Who?"[19]

This will be my way of concluding. To make this unusual link clear, I suggest we juxtapose:

The West-II-Town And Country
1
The body had been buried face downwards.
Only the skeleton was left,
and it separated in handling
when dug up
The coat was yellow ducking,
lined with a light-colored blanket;
overalls of yellow ducking, too,
and a patch on the knee:
a belt on the skeleton,
a knife in the pocket,
and a bullet hole
in the back of the skull.

Testimony I: 93

and,

Tony, still living, was able to drag himself to the bank.
Here he was seen by men on a passing steamboat
and picked up
to live a while longer—and tell what had happened.

Testimony II: 221

and Primo Levi's dream of a survivor who tries to tell his camp experience but discovers the absence of an "*addressable* other," the anguish of "the ever-repeated scene of the unlistened-to story" (Levi 52):

the absence of an *addressable other,* [the absence of] ... an empathic listener. . . an other who can hear the anguish of one's memories and thus affirm and recognize their realness, annihilates the story. And it is, precisely, this ultimate annihilation of a narrative that, fundamentally, *cannot be heard* and of a story that *cannot be witnessed,* which constitutes the mortal eighty-first blow ... [beyond the eighty blows that a man, in Jewish tradition, can sustain and survive] (Felman and Laub 68)

It is my view that Reznikoff's role is to be this "addressable other," [a]"*second degree witness* (witness of witnesses, witness of the testimonies)" (Felman and Laub 213), or the witness of the witness who disappeared.[20] So that, despite all that De Man called "this defacement of the mind" (Felman and Laub 153) there should be someone to give a voice to voiceless suffering. What Maurice Blanchot called *un rhapsode* (572) or what Walter Benjamin called "the task of the translator" might be the witness of the witness who disappeared. This testimonial stance is poetical, because poetry is the locus of a fathering process, a process of words inseminating words (in Hebrew *Zakhor,* memory is related to *Zekhar,* semen). This inseminating process is at the heart of many poems, like *Inscriptions, 1944:*

Where was the Mishnah written?
In Palestine
where bands of Jews had fought against the legions
until Jewish slaves were so many
a Jewish slave was not worth as much as a horse
. . .
so, at the destruction of the Temple
... ten thousand synagogues
took root and flourished
in Palestine and in Babylonia and along the Mediterranean;
so the tides carried from Spain and Portugal

a Spinoza to Holland
and a Disraeli to England.
. . .
One man escapes from the ghetto of Warsaw
. . .
from that man
shall spring again a people
as the sands of the sea for number,
as the stars of the sky.
. . .
and out of the dead body of the lion of Judah,
the prophecies and the psalms;
out of the slaves in Egypt,
. . .
out of the ghettos of Spain and Portugal, Germany and Poland,
the Torah and the prophecies
the Talmud and the sacred studies, the hymns and songs of the
    Jews;
. . .
out of the wounded a people of physicians;
and out of those who met only with hate,
a people of love, a compassionate people.

The Complete Poems II:60

or *The Lionhearted:*

What became of David is, likewise, uncertain. He may have practised
medicine in Lincoln, in London, or even in Lynn. A line or two of
his verse, for it is certain that he did write verse and in Hebrew, too,
until his death, may be in the prayer books of the Jews to this day,
perhaps to introduce a psalm by the greater David or just for one of
the holidays and read only once a year. (*The Lionhearted* 242)

It is not a haphazard coincidence that biological growth and
poetical reactivation, exile and dissemination converge:

Of all that I have written
you say: "how much was poorly said."
But look!
The oak has many acorns
that a single oak might live.

Complete Poems II: 209

Free Verse
Not like flowers in the city
in neat rows or in circles

> but like dandelions
> scattered on a lawn.
>
> *Complete Poems* II: 210 or 115

One may think that nothing warrants this fathering process. And it is my very personal feeling that this remains a religious assertion, an epistemological coup de force, because as Reznikoff said of Judaism:

> I shall walk better in these heavy boots
> than barefoot.
>
> *Complete Poems* II: 25

The whole issue of readability and unreadability, intelligibility and communication thus must be addressed in terms of an ethical leap into action, a *"leap of action,"* being Abraham Heschel's definition of Judaism (81).[21] For Reznikoff it is a leap into writing. The dissemination of speech, which Blanchot called "l'exigence d'une parole fragmentaire" (525), "une parole en archipels," allows "what was said here" to be "heard there." But now along Rorty's lines which alter our Hasids' earlier perspective:

> There ... are two ways of thinking about various things.—The first ... thinks of truth as a vertical relationship between representations and what is represented. The second ... thinks of truth horizontally—as the culminating reinterpretation of our predecessors' reinterpretation of their predecessors' reinterpretation. ... It is the difference between regarding truth, goodness, and beauty as eternal objects which we try to locate and reveal, and regarding them as artefacts whose fundamental design we often have to alter. (*Rhetoric* 221)

Notes

1. Ever since Louis Zukofsky's appreciative comments appeared in *Poetry* (1930), Reznikoff has either been ignored or thought of as a disciple of Pound, never fully maturing out of Ezra Pound's overwhelming orbit. Or, as an Objectivist, he was forever a prisoner of a pioneering group whose reaction against Imagism paved the way to poetic Modernism. Reznikoff, a promising young figure, disappears with Objectivism, when other major poets emerge, specifically William Carlos Williams. The concept of the 1930s Poetic Renaissance has trapped Reznikoff in the depths of the origins of poetic modernism.
2. Louis Zukofsky wrote on the "Limp wet blanket pentameters":

One's got to modernize
His lute
Not by one variation after another,
Our words form a new city,
Ours is no Mozart's
Magic Flute. (*A*)

3. Reznikoff's "three rules in writing prose or verse":

first and above all to be clear, because communication is the purpose of writing (as of speaking); then, to write in rhythm, because that adds to the meaning, as well as the beauty, of speech; and finally to be concise, because that adds to the beauty, as well as the effectiveness, of speech. As for clarity, this seems no longer fashionable in some contemporary writing: the cryptic, I suppose, is. (Perhaps this is an extension or a legacy of the Symbolist doctrine: to suggest is to create; to name is to destroy.) (*First, there is the Need* 5)

4. See T. Todorov: *Le geste constitutif de la poétique est de refuser la transitivité de la littérature et d'instituer cette dernière comme objet de connaissance autonome.* (Kerbrat-Orecchioni 221)
5. George Perec's *Approches de quoi?*

Interroger l'habituel. . . . Comment parler de ces "choses communes," comment les traquer plutôt, comment les débusquer, les arracher à la gangue dans laquelle elles restent engluées, comment leur donner un sens, une langue: qu'elles parlent enfin de ce qui est, de ce que nous sommes.
    Peut-être s'agit-il de fonder enfin notre propre anthropologie. . . . Non plus l'exotique, mais l'endotique. . . . (Kerbrat-Orecchioni 146)

6. Which sends us back to our Hasids' earlier dialogue. Educated in both Hebrew and the Talmud, they conceived of language as infinitely signifying. They belonged to a hermeneutical tradition which held that a word is always more than a word and glorified King David's psalm "Elohim spoke once, twice I heard Him."

Pour les maîtres du Talmud, il existe un rapport quasi ontologique entre l'homme et le texte. La vitalité de l'humain dépend de sa capacité à interpréter le texte. La pratique herméneutique n'est pas seulement une technique, un outil du savoir; elle est véritablement une catégorie existentielle. (Ouaknin 193)

7. White's epigraph to The *Content of the Form*: "Le fait n'a jamais qu'une existence linguistique." Barthes.
8. Should *Holocaust* and *Testimony* be read as twin "documentary poems" (Shevelow 301)? Hardly so. The *Holocaust* reading contract does not mention fictionality: "All that follows is based on a United States government publication, *Trials of the Criminals before the Nuernberg Military Tribunal* and the records of the Eichmann trial in Jerusalem." Nor does it offer soothing New Testament quotations for detached reading. Reznikoff-the historian never failed to distinguish between right and wrong. The teleology is clear since we can only read *Holocaust* in the light of the well-known Nuremberg verdict. The reading horizon marks off Jews as victims and Nazis as victimizers proved guilty.
Second, the relation to the hypotext is dramatically different: Reznikoff did not focus on narrative manipulations. He used a chronological thread from

massacres to mass extermination. *Holocaust* is more "diachronic and processionary," while *Testimony* is "synchronic and static" (*Metahistory* 10). Besides, "narrative tactics" (7) may look alike but Reznikoff's stance is different: in *Holocaust* Reznikoff provided scholarly editing in case the reader's prior historical knowledge might be wanting. He anticipated if not revisionism at least a watering down of historical data. Reznikoff stood on the side of memory.

Third, the ending is structurally different. *Testimony* "does not so much conclude as terminate" (White). Narrative chains await potential reactivation. *Holocaust,* however, is limited to and structurally ends with the unique trial. *Holocaust* narrative reactivation is unlikely.

Fourth, each conclusion has a different weight: *Testimony* is a nonconcluding, arbitrarily-stopped discourse refusing a metaphysical message. *Holocaust's* last poems assert Jewish resistance and survival and vouch for a world in which good is recognizable from evil. Moral values, temporarily negated by Nazism, resurface in an "Aufhebung" of chaos. Compare this to Claude Lanzmann's *Shoah* :

> You know, this was a real question, the question of the end. I did not have the moral right to give a happy ending to this story. When does the *Holocaust* really end? Did it end the last day of the war? Did it end with the creation of the State of Israel? No. It still goes on. These events are of such magnitude, of such scope that they have never stopped developing their consequences.... When I really had to conclude I decided that I did not have the right to do it. And I decided that the last image of the film would be a rolling train, an endlessly rolling ... train.(Felman and Laub 241–42)

Lastly, the issue of witnessing and testimony are addressed by *Testimony*, and *Holocaust*. But *Holocaust* is mainly a book of remembrance, the "Yiskerbiher" of a Jew who did not experience the war, but as "witness through the Imagination" (Kremer) lays claim to this event, takes responsibility and attests to the reality of "an event without a witness" (Felmann and Laub 211). In short, the witness of the dead witness "to an utterly proofless event" (211)

9. Milton Hindus termed this epigraph: "secular scripture."

10. Despite Reznikoff's disclaimer: "I was only a miner and refiner of the metal there" (Shevelow 291). Robert Franciosi showed how Reznikoff processed original court testimonies into poems.(Franciosi 195–244)

11. Genette's hypertextuality defined as: "toute relation unissant un texte B (que j'appellerai *hypertexte*) à un texte antérieur A (que j'appellerai bien sûr *hypotexte*) sur lequel il se greffe d'une manière qui n'est pas celle du commentaire."(13)

12. Out of 528 pages, only fifteen poems include a verdict: in *Testimony* I: 123, 128, 135, 136, 154, and 213; all stressing the uselessness of a racially biased judicial system; in *Testimony* II: 22, 30, 37, 89, 123, 193, 203, 204, and 221, underscoring the fallibility of the judiciary. Such partiality to mainstream whites and bosses is even more significant because it is an implicit indictment of what justice is not.

13. E.g.: a trusting rich father called Lear is betrayed by an ungrateful son.(*Testimony* II: 201)

14. A testimony implies a narrator who is a character in his own narrative, both actor in and narrator of events. Reznikoff skilfully evaded this narratological aporia: how can anyone be actor and narrator, guilty but presumed innocent?

15. This may account for the critical rejection of *Testimony*. Critics ex-

pecting a clear moral message end up blaming Reznikoff for relishing blood, or doubt his mental sanity "in his old age":

> [on *Testimony*] This is not, I think, the reflection of any sixties radical view of America but of a mind that had brooded much on American history and had finally come to be obsessed with its destructiveness, mesmerized by images of maiming and killing. *Holocaust* bears exactly the same relation to recent Jewish history ... there is finally a numbing pointlessness in the constant repetition of savagery and murder without the slightest interpretive response on the part of the poet... One is ultimately led to suspect that this is an extended exercise in masochism conducted under the cover of an act of testimony. History it would seem had become a hypnotic vision of unrestrained murderous impulse for the poet ... in these two long poems of his old age. (Alter 131–32)

Or else, Reznikoff is blamed for an absence of moral vision: he is accused of equalizing the truths of the victims with those of their victimizers, since all testimonies are said to have an equal narrative status.(Sidra DeKoven Ezrahi, in Franciosi 207). That Reznikoff's authorial presence/absence should be both conspicuous and devoid of a moral message is read as a poetical flaw.

Another approach uses the reader-as-jury metaphor, akin to the cathartic effect theory. These are debatable notions, as they confuse hypo and hypertexts. The poems are no vicarious trials. The issue is not: did you come, as a reader, to the same conclusions as the jury? As for catharsis, Reznikoff never begged for readers' identifications with characters. Generic manipulations aim to destabilize identification. Besides, who reads *Testimony* or *Holocaust* feeling purged of passions?

16. The general lack of causal or consequential connections between poems does not preclude the possibility of fragmented cross connections. The reader may link disjointed episodes: e.g., *Samaritan* in *Testimony* II:119–20, and *Testimony* II:199. The same could be done with episodes concerning Indians or Blacks, in the North, South, or West. But what is to be learnt from those connections? A search for meaningful causal connections is frustrated.

17. My analysis in: "D'une Main-Forte: Judéité et écriture poétique dans l'oeuvre de Charles Reznikoff" *Ecriture Poétique Moderne*. Clermont-Ferrand University Press, 1992, 189–214.

18. Non-metaphysical in the sense that Reznikoff challenges a traditional premise of literature ("the traditional claim of the humanities to be a repository of universal wisdom" (Graff 171)), since no truth lies in what is said, and the focus is shifted from message to form. *Testimony*'s status as fiction calls the claims to truth value and realism into question.

19. The title of Primo Levi's 1986 novel *Se Nom Ora, Quando?* And the Song of the Jewish Partisans: "If I'm not for myself, who will be for me? / If not this way, how? If not now, when?"

20. In *Dans la langue de personne, Poésie yiddish de l'anéantissement.*, Paris: Seuil, 1993), R. Ertel used Felman's concept: "Après l'anéantissement, qui est le témoin du témoin absent-sinon le poète?," then quoted J. Derrida: "Le poète est devenu une sorte de narrateur général: au moment de la signature, il s'appelle le témoin (*martyroï, testimonium*)."(33)

21. "A Jew is asked to take a *leap of action* rather than a *leap of thought*."

Works Cited

Alter, Robert. "Poet of Exile" *Commentary*. February 1977: 49–55.

Barthes, Roland. "Littérature littérale" *Essais critiques*. Paris: Seuil, 1964.

Blanchot, Maurice. *L'Entretien infini.* Paris: Gallimard, 1969.

Buber, Martin. *Tales of the Hasidim Later Masters.* 2 vols. New York: Schocken Books, 1974.

Felman, Shoshana, and Laub, Dori. *Testimony, Crises of Witnessing in Literature, Psychoanalysis, and History.* New York: Routledge, 1992.

Fish, Stanley. *Doing What Comes Naturally, Change Rhetoric and the Practice of Theory in Literature and Legal Studies.* Oxford: Clarendon, 1989.

———. "Rhetoric." Frank Lentricchia and Thomas McLaughlin, eds. *Critical Terms for Literary Study.* Chicago: University of Chicago Press, 1990: 163–76.

Franciosi, Robert Michael. A *Story of Vocation: The Poetic Achievement of Charles Reznikoff.* Diss. University of Iowa, 1985. Ann Arbor: University of Michigan, 1985. 85 18828.

Gelpi, Albert. *A Coherent Splendor the American Poetic Renaissance 1910–1950.* Cambridge: Cambridge University Press, 1987; 1990.

Genette, Gérard. *Palimpsestes, la littérature au second degré.* Paris: Seuil, 1982.

Graff, Gerald. "Determinacy/Indeterminacy," Frank Lentricchia and Thomas McLaughlin, eds. *Critical Terms for Literary Study.* Chicago: University of Chicago Press, 1990: 163–76.

Gray, Richard. *American Poetry of the Twentieth Century.* London: Longman, 1991.

Habermas, Jürgen. *La penseé postmétaphysique. Essais philosophiques.* Trans. Rainer Rochlitz. Paris: Colin, 1993.

Heschel, Abraham Joshua. *Between God and Man,* edited by Fritz A. Rothschild, New York: 1959.

Hindus, Milton, ed. *Charles Reznikoff, Man and Poet.* National Poetry Foundation: University of Maine, Orono. 1984.

Kerbrat-Orecchioni, Catherine. *L'énonciation, de la subjectivité dans le langage.* Paris: Colin, 1980.

Levi, Primo. *Survival in Auschwitz.* Translated by Stuart Woolf. New York: Macmillan, 1961.

Ouaknin, Marc-Alain. *Concerto pour quatre consonnes sans voyelles.* Paris: Balland, 1991.

Reznikoff, Charles. *First, there is the Need.* Santa Barbara: Black Sparrow, 1977.

———. *Holocaust.* Los Angeles: Black Sparrow, 1975.

———. *Testimony a Recitative.* 2 vols. Santa Barbara: Black Sparrow, 1979.

———. *The Complete Poems 1918–1975.* Santa Rosa: Black Sparrow, 1989.

———. *The Lionhearted A Story About The Jews in Medieval England* Philadelphia: The Jewish Publication Society of America, 5704–1944.

———. *The Jews of Charleston A History of an American Jewish Community.* With the collaboration of Uriah Z. Engelman. Philadelphia: The Jewish Publication Society of America, 5711–1950.

Shevelow, Kathryn. "History and Objectification in Charles Reznikoff's Documentary Poems, *Testimony* and *Holocaust" Sagetrieb*, vol. 1, no. 2, Fall 1982: 290–306.

White, Hayden. *The Content of the Form, Narrative Discourse and Historical Representation.* Baltimore: The Johns Hopkins University Press, 1987.

———. *Metahistory, The Historical Imagination in Nineteenth-Century Europe.* Baltimore: The Johns Hopkins University Press, 1973, 1990.

Tato Laviera's Nuyorican Poetry:
The Choice of Bilingualism

VÉRONIQUE RAULINE AND TATO LAVIERA

THERE IS SOMETHING GOING ON IN *THE AMERICAS!* IN MUSIC, LITERA-
ture, and the visual arts, new voices are emerging, challenging
traditional patterns and developing in new ways and new para-
digms. Names have been coined to try and grasp this current
movement: *Nuyorican* is one of them.

A combination of New York and Puerto Rican, Nuyorican has
been used for the past twenty years to refer to Puerto Ricans,
either born or raised in the States, or residing there on a more-
or-less permanent basis. The term was coined in the 70s by
two Nuyorican poets, Miguel Piñero and Miguel Algarín, and was
intended to signify a specific Nuyorican experience within the
United States. What has come to be labeled Nuyorican literature
is both an explicit testimony to and an assertion of this experience. Intimately related to the Puerto Ricans' colonial history,
to their specific social, economic and cultural environment in
the US and to the debate on acculturation, or "assimilation,"
Nuyorican literature represents both the outcome of such historical processes and a response to them. Migrating to the United
States in 1960, Tato Laviera has been part and parcel of this
movement and is a major representative of the Nuyorican literary scene.

This paper was given by Véronique Rauline and Tato Laviera in dialogue
form. The texts or poems read by Tato Laviera in the oral presentation are
indented in the written text and their references are given in parentheses
with abbreviations referring to Tato Laviera's four books of poems as follows:

C : *La Carreta Made a U-Turn*, Houston, Arte Público, 1992 (1980).
E : *Enclave*, Houston, Arte Público, 1981.
A : *AmeRícan*, Houston, Arte Público, 1984.
M : *Mainstream Ethics*, Houston, Arte Público, 1988.

New York Puerto Rican Literature

New York Puerto Rican literature in two languages/three forms, Spanish, Spanglish and English, abounds inside the *callejones* of New York. Literature deep in embroidered richness, vernaculars of Indian Jíbaros inside Black English talk, centered in classical Spanish verses, three political ideologies—statehood, commonwealth and independence—all actively pursuing the Boricua land in diversified poetic expression. Literature of urban, brick-cold minority realities: literature of music, growing and strong; literature of motherhood as determined as ever; literature called development; forward, fast-tongued, struggling to keep afloat. All in all, New York Latino literature, ready to gain control, meaning literary movement is vibrant, eighty-achieving, oral, de boca, emerging from the soul-gut experiences de nuestra gente, pa'arriba, pa'alante, ¡qué vale![1]

Nuyorican, Chicano, Creoleness . . . : these names signal the forging of new identities for entire peoples whose history has been one of negation, uprooting, transplantation, and exile; or rather, they signal the will to baptize such identities "perhaps still in the making, but nevertheless real."[2] Although each has its own specificities, all these names and the positioning they reveal point to the issue of choice. They choose to refuse the simplistic either / or alternative. They offer an escape from the neither / nor (or in-between) downgrading reserved to those who refuse to be culturally maimed.

> we gave birth to a new generation,
> AmeRícan, broader than lost gold
> never touched, hidden inside
> the puerto rican mountains.

These names enhance these peoples' composite nature, their "diversality," and voice the need to investigate this *mestizo* aggregate, as *one, uno,* a specific albeit provisional identity, made up of *all* but being *none.*

> we gave birth to a new generation,
> AmeRícan, it includes everything
> imaginable you-name-it-we-got-it
> society.

we gave birth to a new generation,
AmeRícan salutes all folklores,
european, indian, black, spanish,
and anything else compatible.

This new generation proclaimed by the poet was born in New
York, and from a deictic point of view, Tato Laviera's poetry is
definitely New York urban-based. Yet, bringing the island to the
metropolis, his poems successfully transcend the original split
between the *here-New York* and *there-Puerto Rico*. The to-and-
fro metaphor of air traveling between these two symbolic places
is reexplored by Laviera in order to open up new poetic airlifts.

AmeRícan, across forth and across back
back across and forth back
forth across and back and forth
our trips are walking bridges!

it all dissolved into itself, the attempt
was truly made, the attempt was truly
absorbed, digested, we spit out
the poison, we spit out the malice,
we stand, affirmative in action,
to reproduce a broader answer to the
marginality that gobbled us up abruptly!

This broader answer starts from the basic assumption—
shared by a great many Caribbeans and Latin Americans, either
at home or in the metropolis—that defining one's self should
not mean facing multiple-choice questions with only one "right"
answer—a caricature of which is the racial questionnaire in U.S.
censuses, giving headaches to many every ten years!—but rather,
a single multiple-answer or multi-faceted-answer question: "who
are we?"

AmeRícan, walking plena-rhythms in new york,
strutting beautifully alert, alive,
many eyes wondering,
admiring!

AmeRícan, defining myself my own way any way many
says Am e Rícan, with the big R and the
accent on the í!

For those who choose to go their own way, their commitment
is therefore "to set in motion the expression of what we are."

Formulated by three writers from the French Caribbean in a text entitled *In Praise of Creoleness*,[3] this commitment is echoed in Laviera's expressed intention "to reflect the globality of the Puerto Rican essence," by exploring and working all the shades of his "rainbow people." This is first and foremost visible at the linguistic level:

> AmeRícan, speaking new words in spanglish tenements,
>   fast tongue moving street corner "que
>   corta" talk being invented at the insistence
>   of a smile!
>
> (*A*, 94)

and best exemplified in his bilingual technique.

As Tato Laviera put it: "I'm trying to cross linguistically to reflect the nature of my people." As the everyday experiences of the Puerto Ricans in New York are:

> the source, the strength,
> the base of my inspirations
>
> (*C*, 13)

the linguistic habits most common in the community are the basis of his poetic language. Indeed, Laviera runs the gamut of the Puerto Ricans' linguistic behaviors and speech varieties, inhabits all their registers and "branches out," as Juan Flores put it, with other "bro talks," sounds, or rhythms. He evolves his own speech out of this compost:

> black american soul english talk
> with native plena sounds
> and primitive urban salsa beats
>
> (*M*, 27)

It has often been noted that while bi-or multilingual, authors are not usually polyglot *as writers*. That is why describing Laviera's poetry as "fully" or "integrally" bilingual, as Juan Flores did, is highly significant, for bilingual researching is the core of his poetry and poetics.[4]

Speakers in the New York Puerto Rican community range from Spanish monolinguals to English monolinguals, but the overwhelming majority are bilinguals and tend to use both Spanish and English, separately and in a mixed form in their everyday colloquial speech. These "two languages/three forms" have always been represented and virtually evenly distributed in Laviera's work. Without embarking into a detailed count, English, Spanish and bilingual poems appear as balanced in his books. But this balance is defined by the poet as "competitive," reminding us that what we traditionally call "language contact" is very often a euphemism to refer to a genuine linguistic battle, imposed on colonized peoples through politically motivated linguistic planning and policies.

The bilingual condition thus provides the poet with a thematic concern resulting in a very sharp metalinguistic discourse: commenting upon the relationship between two different languages within a single individual or community, it addresses the so-called "bilingual issue," which Laviera cannot evade both as a speaker and as a poet.

my graduation speech

i think in spanish
i write in english

i want to go back to puerto rico,
but i wonder if my kink could live
in ponce, mayagüez and carolina

tengo las venas aculturadas
escribo en spanglish
abraham in español
abraham in english
tato in spanish
"taro" in english
tonto in both languages

how are you?
¿cómo estás?
i don't know if i'm coming
or si me fui ya

si me dicen barranquitas, yo reply,
"¿con qué se come eso?"
si me dicen caviar, i digo,
"a new pair of converse sneakers."

ahí supe que estoy jodío
ahí supe que estamos jodíos

english or spanish

spanish or english
spanenglish
now, dig this:

hablo lo inglés matao
hablo lo español matao
no sé leer ninguno bien

so it is, spanglish to matao
what i digo
            ¡ay, virgen, yo no sé hablar!

                                              (*C*, 17)

   Although recently linguistic research has produced works
concentrating on the advantages of being bilingual, bilingualism
has often been viewed as a crippling handicap, to the extent
that it sometimes came to mean possessing not *two* but *less
than one* language. Code-switching in particular, the alternate
use of two languages within speech—and especially intra-
sentential code-switching, the alternate use of two languages
within a single sentence—has been broadly used with a derogatory connotation, and code-switchers have often been considered as unable to speak either language. From their positions of
bi -linguals, they were downgraded to that of *semi* -lingual or
a -lingual speakers.
   Laviera's poem "my graduation speech," exploits the seemingly
random linguistic alternation for humoristic purposes, much in
the same way as 'macaronic' poetry. It thereby delivers a direct
and ironic response to this trend that I would call *linguistic
monocentrism,* which has led to considering monolingualism
as the norm, the rule, and bilingualism as the deviance. It also
points to the freedom of the poet who is entitled to assert along
with Jean-Paul Sartre in *L'Être et le néant: Je ne puis être infirme sans me choisir infirme* ["I will be crippled only if I choose
to be so"]. Hence the poems' ability to defy linguistic, psycholin-
guistic, and sociolinguistic grids of analysis, or rather to embrace
them all. None is wrong, but all are only partly relevant and
prove unable to account for the totality of Laviera's bilingualism.
   At the individual level for instance, bilingualism is the generally accepted term describing one's ability to use two different
languages. But this broad definition does not express the various
ways to perform one's dual linguistic competence. From the use
of one nonintegrated loanword into a monolingual instance of
discourse to complex intra-sentential code-switching, there is a

wide spectrum, as wide as that covered by Laviera's poetic voice whose competence, as noted by Frances Aparicio, may vary from one poem to the next for esthetic or thematic purposes.

Similarly, bilingual studies have attempted to specify, for each situation, the relationship existing between the languages at play. This has mainly consisted in introducing new concepts to say what the term bilingualism, simply pointing to a linguistic duality, did not say about the organization of such duality. Some sociolinguists, for instance, have distinguished between bilingualism and diglossia. The latter term has been reserved for those situations when each language is used to perform specialized social functions. A diglossic analysis of Laviera's poetry would then aim at showing that the distribution of Spanish and English in his poems is highly compartmentalized, culturally and emotionally exclusive.

Some poems do operate around the isolation of Spanish and English to specific domains. This is mostly true for those monolingual poetic instances when words in the other language are used to illustrate dual surroundings and to signify a deictic, or emotional, shift. For instance:

> te digo que el welfare me debe pagar overtime
>
> (*E*, 28)

or:

> good. he took it all,
> but he left me intact,
> but i know he lives in the neighborhood.
> the network of our bodega, barbería, bakeries
> will identify el canalla.
>
> (*M*, 28)

As pointed out by several critics and researchers, a diglossic analysis may also apply to the poem entitled "a sensitive bolero in transformation." The encounter between English and Spanish is centered on the opposition of the phonetic outlook of the Spanish word "seno" and its supposed English equivalent, "breast," this opposition being materialized at the graphic level.

> se no
> se no
>   breast
>   breast

        se sensual
        no se
        suspiro
                breast
                hard
                duro
                mistreated
                maltratado
                manoseado

The poem ends in an ultimate confrontation between the two
languages, the Spanish sibilant and nasal consonants and the
English plosives:

        seno sensual
        seno orgánico
                why then
                do you treat them
                just as breasts?
                                        (C, 38)

But such a division of linguistic tasks does not hold for all
poems. In the poem entitled "standards," for instance, the physical experience of softness is exclusively rendered in English:

                so suave, touch,
                so smooth, touch, touch,
                sweet
                smells
                sensored
                sensual
                sensations
                saturated
                softly
                smoothly
                seducing
                sensitive
                stems
                slowly
                                        (E, 48)

Indeed, Laviera's bilingualism is far from being exclusive. Code-
switching does enable him, at times, to highlight linguistic frontiers. But it is also his major tool to try and blur them. If Laviera

builds bridges, the major movement of his poetry does not consist in going from one side to the other but rather in standing *on* the bridge, walking it. This positioning is far-reaching. The interactive plurality it launches, enables the language confrontation suppressed by compartmentalized diglossic schemes to resurface in his poems and to threaten, undermine not only monolingual minimalism but language itself.[5]

Drawing frontiers and abolishing them: such figures as repetition, iteration, and contrast, whose creative potential are renewed and expanded by the bilingual material of the poet, proceed from both. The 'bilingual doublet' for instance, or the repetition of one meaning in two languages is used by Laviera in various poems. In some stanzas of 'jesús papote' (*E*, 12)—a ten page poem which has come to be identified as the epic poem of Nuyorican life—Laviera resorts to bilingual doublets as a kind of rhythmic leitmotiv. In two instances:

> cold-frío
> hope-esperanza

the two signifiers are linked by a hyphen that may be said to symbolize both the distance separating them and the possibility to cover this distance and even to unite the signifiers through a device of bilingual word-formation. In other instances of the same poem, language appears to get rid of the hyphen checkpoint and to generate its own *ad lib* repetition:

> veins venas veins venas
> the fix la cura the fix la cura cura cura

The strategy of discourse here is obvious: bilingual repetition further stresses what is meant or expressed, in itself or combined to monolingual repetition or iteration, as illustrated in the poem "pana" (*A*, 50):

> i was in jail, brother, jail, brother.
> encarcelao, under, bro, allá adentro,
> solo, alone, bro, all by myself,
> even with another name;

La critique ne retranche pas, elle ne supprime pas, elle ajoute, wrote Barthes in an article on Brecht.[6] ["Criticizing something doesn't amount to cutting anything off it, or abolishing it, but rather to adding to it."] Fighting the dominant discourse (or language) does not mean reducing it to an abridged version but amplifying it, saturating it, exposing it through repetition.

"Brava" (*A,* 63). A Nuyorican woman is being criticized. The criticism, repetitive, monotonous is centered around the language issue, the relation of the Puerto Rican diaspora to English, Spanish, and bilingualism.

> they kept on telling me
> "tú eres disparatera"
> they kept on telling me
> "no se entiende"
> they kept on telling me
> "habla claro, speak spanish"
> they kept on telling me
> telling me, telling me

"They kept on telling me": the repetition leads to a direct illustration of the iterative lexical aspect of the verb "to keep on." The "puertorriqueña" thus criticized then comes to "speech blows."

> and so, the inevitable
> my spanish arrived
> "tú quieres que yo hable
> en español" y le dije
> all the spanish words
> in the vocabulary,
> you know which ones, los que
> cortan, and then i proceeded
> to bilingualize it,

The bilingual speech she delivers seems generated by the same device: repeating, hammering out, rapping out words, as if in order to be understood; it was not enough to utter a word once, but it had to be repeated. As if twice was the rule:

> i know
> yo sé that que you know
> tú sabes que yo soy that
> i am puertorriqueña in
> english

The formation of this passage could arbitrarily be traced back in three stages, each of them removing nothing but adding something. First, recursiveness, expressed in each language:

> i know that you know that i am . . .
> yo se que tú sabes que yo soy . . .

Then, code-switching, which introduces an ontological polarity switch on the verb *ser*/to be:

> i know that you know que yo soy.
> yo sé que tú sabes that i am.

Finally, the merging of the two lines, redundantly:

> i know yo sé that que you know tú sabes
> que yo soy that i am puertorriqueña in english

The poem starts with a tight separation of the two codes to illustrate the lack of understanding, or rather the unwillingness to understand. It then moves towards the merging of Spanish and English. First experienced as duplication, mirroring, the merging then freely develops, improvises around the figure of repetition.

> and there's nothing
> you can do but to accept
> it como yo soy sabrosa
> proud ask any streecorner
> where pride is what you defend
> go ahead, ask me, on any street-
> corner that i am not puertorriqueña,
> come díme lo aquí- en mi cara
> offend me, atrévete, a menos
> que tú no quieras que yo te meta
> un tremendo bochinche de soplamoco
> pezcozá that's gonna hurt you
> in either language, así que
> no me jodas mucho, y si me jodes
> keep it to yourself, a menos
> que te quieras arriesgar
> y encuentres and you find
> pues, que el cementerio
> está lleno de desgracias
> prematuras, ¿estás claro?
> are you clear? the cemetery
> is full of premature short-
> comings.

What is implied here is no longer moving from one language to the other, but mixing the two. The result of such a mixture was described by Juan Bruce-Novoa as "interlingual" because: "the two languages are put into a state of tension which produces a third, an 'inter' possibility of language."[7] How could this "inter-possibility of language" be characterized?

In most interlingual instances, the semantic meaning and syntactic structure, although not as transparent as in the case of monolingualism, can easily be reconstructed. Yet, and especially when the poem is read aloud, there remains the feeling that, at one point, language gave way, the feeling that something hiding beneath language and that its structure tries to conceal, emerged. An impression of destabilization, when you feel something that outweighs what is being said and in what language. A physical experience of language. A political one too.

In an attempt to account for this destabilization, Puerto Rican and Chicano scholars have proposed to resort to the concept of "foregrounding" as the main effect produced by literary code-switching. Coined by the prewar Prague Linguistic School, foregrounding was defined as "the use of the devices of the language in such a way that this use itself attracts attention and is perceived as uncommon."[8] Along this line, code-switching appears as a poetic device in and by itself and "foregrounding" as a generic concept to integrate the various bilingual strategies at work in literature.

Foregrounding raises interesting questions when two or more languages are involved. Mukarovsky, for instance, explained that the background against which the foregrounded instance is projected may either be the standard and/or the esthetic canon. These remain valid for bilingual poetry. But its background comprises an additional feature: the linguistic canon, which considers the mixing of two languages as abnormal, or deviant. Bilingual literature may also foreground in relation to the bilingual canon, that is to say, deviate from the syntactical rules and constraints that have been found to apply in community switching. Combining them all, Laviera's poetic structure is "revealed as a concert of fores."[9]

savorings, from piñones to loíza

to combine the smell of tropical
plaintain rootssofritoed
into tasty crispy platanustres
after savoring a soft mofongo
with pork rind pieces, before
you cooked them into an escabeche

peppered with garlic tostones
at three o'clock in a piñones sunday afternoon, after your body cre-
mated itself dancing the night, madrugando
in san juan beaches, walking over
a rooster's cucu rucu and pregonero's
offering of wrapped-up alcapurrias
fried in summer sun ...
hold yourself strong
ahead is the Ancón, the crossing to loíza ...
you have entered the underneath
of plena, mi hermano,
steady rhythms that constantly dont change
steady rhythms that constantly dont change
tru cu tú   tru cu tú
tru cu tú   tru cu tú
tu tu tu

(C, 59)

"A concert of fores." The reference to the musical field here
provides us with a new path to try and run across such interactive heterogeneity. If linguistic analyses fail to integrate all its
facets, this may be because one element resists their method:
rhythm, which may be worth exploring as the dominant in Laviera's poetry.

hispano

un
 vals
  en
   vallenato
   picoteando
    samba
     merengueada
      con
       ranchera
        de
        mambo
         combinada
          en
           salsa
           de
            plena
             polka
              rumbeando

```
                              bolero
                          a
                           la
                          cha
                            cha
                             cha
                              chi
                               cha
                                peruana
                                 cumbia
          folklórica
            bomba
            y
              guaracha
              picaíta
              seis
                de
                    andino
                    danza
                    mezclada
                      en
                        baladas
                        nocturnas
                        de
                         tango
                         son
                         de
                           unotodos
                           todosuno
                            pasitos
                            unidos
                             a la
                                vuelta
                                del
                                 compás.
```
(M, 47)

As suggested by Juan Flores, because Laviera "activates all the various strains of the native Puerto Rican oral tradition" the bridges laid down in his poems are also rhythmic ones. "Songs in the key of the many people with whom Tato Laviera seeks to strike up a rhythm,"[10] many poems by Laviera assert the primacy and precedence of rhythm over language, first in relation to Africa, which is:

musically rooted way way back

before any other language.

(C, 43)

As such, his poetry may be viewed as an enactment of what Calvet proposed to call "rhythmic competence."[11] A filter through which language is both "raped," rapped, and revealed, "rhythmic competence," as defined by Calvet, manifests itself through formal patterns but by far exceeds them.

De la voix au geste jusqu'à la peau, tout le corps est actif dans le discours. Mais c'est un corps social, historique autant que subjectif. [From the voice through body language to the skin, the whole body is involved in speech. But this is a social body, as much historical as subjective.] This quote by Meschonnic,[12] illustrates this author's conception of rhythm as the full expression of the movement of speech and the life of language. Integrating the subject's individual and collective history, rhythm may be viewed as a wandering stance able to subsume the rigidity and seriousness of political speech. If dogmatism is defined as the perpetual repetition of the same slogans, analyses, and rhetoric, rhythm seems to act as a powerful prevention against any kind of stereotyped language. It does not tone down the language conflict but projects it on the rhythmic scene.

Consequently, the bilingual voice is not necessarily expressed in a bilingual register. It rises against an environment striving to conceal its power and political, revolutionary impact under some monophonic univocity. Language as such—and not only the linguistic registers of the Nuyoricans—becomes both the battlefield and the weapon of the Nuyorican poet. "Languages are struggling to possess us" said Miguel Algarín. What is needed, therefore, is to strike back with the same weapon, to speak back and write back. This linguistic weapon invested by the community's actors through the poem, as a most faithful extension of "ordinary" bilingualism in the *barrio,* transcends all linguistic barriers—even those laid down by bilingualism.

(...) you don't
need a bilingual dictionary, what i said
can cut in any language

(A, 58)

In the last poem of his latest book, language is described by Tato Laviera as:

la ametralladora de la libertad

[the machine gun of freedom.]

(M, 49)

If language is a weapon, and if it is necessary to grab this weapon to liberate one's self, it is the very role of the poet that is being commented upon.

political

i'm pushed, i'm being pushed, pushed,
i'm pushed, i'm being pushed, pushed,
into the gutter, i'm being pushed,
into boiling point anger,
i'm being pushed, pushed,
yet i retain control,
yet i lean back,
yet i turn the other cheek,
yet i look to god for patience,
i'm being pushed, pushed,
into violent action,
that tells me something,
i must do something i must
contribute to my community,
i must get involved,
i'm pushed, i'm being pushed, pushed,
yet i take alternative roads,
to keep away from the involvement,
because community leadership,
leads to broken marriages,
leads, to lack of trust,
you do and do for the people,
and the people will stab you
in the back, so, i do nothing
but knock on cold steel
with a rubber hammer,
attempting to penetrate,
until my soul no longer sweats,
but then, one day, i heard
music on the other side of
steel and i wrote down
the lyrics, marching with every
beat, shooting bullets of words
i sang the tune with my friends,
malice and injustice pushed again

and i made a citizen's arrest.

(A, 79)

As a linguistic activist, Tato Laviera does not only voice the linguistic confrontation, but the power of words as source of our imprisonment but also of our liberation. His poetry stands as an antidote against:

<table>
<tr><td></td><td>silencio desorientado</td></tr>
<tr><td></td><td>frases mutiladas</td></tr>
<tr><td>maimed sentences</td><td></td></tr>
<tr><td></td><td>sílabas congeladas</td></tr>
<tr><td>frozen syllables</td><td></td></tr>
<tr><td></td><td>silencio desorientado</td></tr>
<tr><td>disoriented silence</td><td></td></tr>
</table>

(M, 49)

The battle is not over, for Puerto Ricans are still "in the commonwealth stage of [their] lives" (A, 80). But the objective is set down. And the last poem in Laviera's latest book can end with this slogan-word:

ganaremos

(M, 49)

Laviera's poetic voice is undoubtedly one that seeks fusion, probably the most extensively used semantic field in his poetry. But in his poetry, just as in jazz, fusion does not necessarily give birth to polyphonic or polyrhythmic convergence. The encounter of various linguistic or musical modes or rhythms sometimes creates disruptive zones that result in creative divergence. Such is probably the price to pay for choosing to write bilingual, for "tempting alien tongues" and "committing the sin of blending"— a price Laviera is more than willing to pay. Because as Jean-Jacques Lecercle pointed out: "We enjoy sinning against language because the violence we impose on its structure is what makes it alive."[13] And Laviera and his language are beautifully alive.

Notes

1. Tato Laviera, Revista Chicano-Riqueña ("New York City Special") 1980.
2. Juan Bruce-Novoa, "A Question of Identity: What's in a Name? Chicanos and Riqueños," in Images and Identities: The Puerto Ricans in Two World Contexts, ed. A. Rodriguez de Laguna (Rio Piedras: Huracán, 1985), 234.

3. Jean Bernabé, Patrick Chamoiseau and Raphaël Confiant, *In Praise of Creoleness* (Paris: Gallimard, 1993), 75.

4. "[Tato Laviera's voice] is integrally bilingual, not just Spanish plus English but an entire fabric of meaning composed of the semantic, phonetic and musical suggestiveness of both." Juan Flores, "Keys to Tato Laviera," Preface to *Enclave* (Houston: Arte Público, 1981), 6.

5. It is worth noting here that diglossia has been used throughout the world to theorize the need to maintain the split between dominant and dominated languages and that Kenyan writer Ngugi wa Thoing'o, for instance, was jailed and exiled for transgressing this established order.

6. Roland Barthes, "Brecht et le discours: contribution á l'étude de la discursivité," in *Le Bruissement de la langue. Essais critiques IV* (Paris: Le Seuil, 1984), 246.

7. Juan Bruce-Novoa, *Question,* 232.

8. Bohuslav Havránek, "The Functional Differentiation of the Standard Language," in *Some Basic and Less Known Aspects of the Prague Linguistic School,* ed. Josef Vachek (Prague: Czechoslovak Academy of Science, 1983), 143–64.

9. Jan Mukarovsky, "Standard Language and Poetic Language," in ibid., 185.

10. Juan Flores, *Keys,* 5.

11. Louis-Jean Calvet, *Pour et contre Saussure* (Paris: Payot, 1975), and *La Production révolutionnaire: slogans, affiches, chansons* (Paris: Payot, 1976).

12. Henri Meschonnic, *Les Etats de la poétique* (Paris: Presses Universitaires de France, collection Ecriture, 1985).

13. Jean-Jacques Lecercle, *The Violence of Language* (London: Routledge, 1990), 10.

Thomas Kinsella and the Poetry
of Irish Difference

TAFFY MARTIN

IDENTIFYING THE VARIETY, THE SCOPE, THE INTRANSIGENCE AND THE ramifications of "difference" as it operates in Thomas Kinsella's poetry is a task that can hardly be separated from the reading of that poetry, for Kinsella's difference is muted and subtle as it is pervasive. He writes in English, translates from Irish, and orchestrates out of the inevitable confrontation between those two worlds a poetry whose very strength is its irresolution.

Having begun with the formal, eminently quotable poems that won him early critical recognition, Kinsella moved on—in a process common to nearly every poet of his generation—to a more open and personal style. With this new style, Kinsella's mythmaking, foreshadowed in the early poems, came to maturity. In these first two manifestations, Kinsella was comprehensible, easy to hear and to like, and eminently "anthologizable." But the poetry that follow is one of originary, often unsettling, violence, most often turned inward toward the poet's own psyche. At the close of this cathartic period, Kinsella returns to his cosmic mythology, incorporating into it the rawness unearthed in his cycle of violence. These last poems have been collected into a volume entitled, quite appropriately, *Blood and Family*. In this 1988 volume and in the poems that have disappeared since that date, Kinsella has become deliberately, almost obsessively, self-referential. Persons, places, and events of the early poems reappear. Certain passages are reworked; some are reprinted unchanged. The personal history and the work itself have come full circle. The result is a remarkable, difficult, and uncompromising body of work, one that sets ancestral voices against the rhythms of everyday speech, flirting with and at the same time criticizing nostalgia. These are poems of psychic mythmaking and profound ambivalence.

164

Troubling Differences

Having published his first poems and gained critical recogniton while working as a civil servant in Ireland's Finance Ministry, Kinsella immortalized his ironic perception of this divided existence in one of his early masterpieces, the poem "Nightwalker," where "a vagabond / Tethered" paces about Dublin haunted by the transmography that will settle upon him at dawn:

> come scratching in our waistcoats
> Down to the kitchen for a cup of tea;
> Then with our briefcases, through wind or rain,
> Past our neighbours' gardens—Melrose, Bloomfield—
> To wait at the station, fluttering our papers.[1]

Caught between the professional paraphernalia of this diurnal existence and the ancestral callings of his psyche, Kinsella will devote himself, as David Lloyd has so perceptively said of Samuel Beckett, "to the thorough and elegant elaboration of the insurmountable contradictions of identity."[2]

At the very heart of those contradictions is Kinsella's love/hate relationship with the English language, a condition similar to that which Dominique Deblaine, in her perceptive analysis of Caribbean diglossia, has identified as *le trouble aimant de la langue*.[3] But while Deblaine sees Aimé Césaire's *Loquèle antillaise* as a liberating watershed for Caribbean postcolonial writers, Kinsella finds only precedent—not comfort—in Yeats's tormented confession:

> I owe my soul to Shakespeare, to Spenser and to Blake, perhaps to William Morris, and to the English language in which I think, speak, and write, [...] everything I love has come to me through English; my hatred tortures me with love, my love with hate.[4]

A victim of that same love/hate relationship, Kinsella defends his much contested decision to write in English by explaining that writing in Irish would be not only artificial but a distortion of the very act of communicating: "Everything that happens to me, happens in English."[5]

This laconic remark, so typical of Kinsella, suggests the subtlety of his linguistic difference and distinguishes him from writers who face a more absolute clash of language. There is nothing, for instance, in his work that even approaches the terror portrayed by Maxine Hong Kingston in her "Song for the Barbarian Reed Pipe" where a Chinese-American schoolgirl responds to the "dumbness" and the "shame" of her linguistic alterity—"my broken voice come skittering out into the open. It makes people wince to hear it."[6]—by tormenting the only classmate whose difference is even more marked than her own. Less confrontational, too, than the *parler hybride*[7] of Chicano poetry, Kinsella's awareness of his difference intensified nonetheless once he left the familiar, albeit stifling surroundings of the Irish civil service. When he arrived in the United States as Writer-in-Residence at the University of Illinois, the Americans he met pronounced his name all wrong, Italianizing it into Kinsella; and when his seminar on the Irish Literary Renaissance turned up in the university catalog under the rubric "Late Nineteenth / Early Twentieth Century British Literature," he refused to teach it.

The Irish Connection

Eloquent but ineffectual, Kinsella's protest situates his difference in a postcolonial context and illustrates what Edward Said has diagnosed as "the power of culture to be an agent of and perhaps the main agency for powerful differentiation."[8] Kinsella readily admits the inviolability of this superior position but refuses to be silenced by it. Instead, he embraces his difference, inscribes it in his poetry and turns his sense of otherness into agency. The central consciousness of the work is that of a poet whose foray into a shadowy Dublin haunted by Joyce leads him to recognize the sheer madness of his undertaking.

> Mindful of the
>   shambles of the day
> But mindful, under the
>   blood's drowsy humming,
> Of will that gropes for
>   structure—nonetheless
> Not unmindful of
>   the madness without,
> The madness within (the
>   book of reason slammed
> Open, slammed shut)
>   we presume to say:

Poems, 101

Mad but mindful, the poet presumes the ultimate: he equates his own ordeal with that of the inevitable master, William Butler Yeats. Responding to periodic attempts to "desacralize" Yeats, Kinsella identifies with his troubling predecessor and imagines for both of them an appropriately noble fate.

> The tireless shadow-eaters
> Close in with tough nose
> And pale fang to expose
> Fibre, weak flesh, speech organs.
> They eat, but cannot eat.
> Dog-faces in his bowels,
> Bitches at his face,
> He grows whole and remote.
>
> *Poems,* 98

Having thus assumed the mantle of poet, Kinsella sets out to explore "the odd blend of rigour and squalor" that constitutes the "imaginative bedrock" of his own, and therefore of Irish, experience. In the pursuit of an all-encompassing myth, he follows history back through his own ancestors, interiorizing the psychic violence he so thoroughly encounters that the image of the poet around which he built his stately 1967 poem, "Mirror in February," cannot but be fractured. "Worker in Mirror, at his Bench," published in 1973 in the wake of his imaginative and formal breakthrough, blurs the distinction between source for and representation of the poet. The image of the craftsman intermingles with that of the artisan/grandfather, both real and mythic, while an ironic nod to Yeats in his tower reifies the strategy of difference:

> Silent rapt surfaces
> assemble glittering
> among themselves.
>
> A few more pieces.
>
> What to call it . . .
> Bright Assembly?
> Foundations for a Tower?
> Open Trap? Circular-Tending
> Self-Reflecting Abstraction . . .[9]

On the one hand, the artist is a genius, and the work he creates testifies to his mastery. On the other, that work might be nothing more than solipsistic nonsense. Kinsella pinpoints the very essence of this creative dilemma in the prefatory essay to his translation of *The Táin*. He admires the mythic dimension of Lady Gregory's version of "Cuchulain of Muirthemne" but regrets the "uneasiness" that led her to excise much of the saga's essential filth and violence.[10] An Irish writer, Kinsella proposes, must temper his "will that gropes for structure" with an ironic appreciation of doctrinaire Irishness. Yeats and Joyce had already shown how to do so.

The Lesson of the Masters

One of the truly comic, but by no means innocent, moments of Yeats's autobiography is his depiction of and meditation upon the exemplary Irishness of his uncle, George Pollexfen. Regaling in the privilege of his Celtic birthright, this enigmatic dreamer "in whom the sap of life seemed to be dried away" lived in a cycle of perpetual despondency, "sighing every twenty-second of June over the shortening of the days" and yet somehow still possessing "a mind full of pictures."[11] As Daniel O'Hara has remarked, the lesson of this contradictory imagination was not lost on the young Yeats, who recognized in his mercurial ancestor's behavior the possibility of cultivating a malleable style, one capable of incorporating into Celtic passion its necessary corrective, irony.[12] Like Yeats, Kinsella would learn how to exploit rather than abide nostalgia.

Once again, Kinsella's forefathers had shown the way. Joyce turns his ambivalence toward the nostalgia for "that Irish thing" into a nonsense passage in *Ulysses* in which a peasant woman who has come to deliver the morning's milk unwittingly plays the straight man to the posturing of a group of students:

> —Is it French you are talking, sir? the old woman said to Haines. Haines spoke to her again in a longer speech, confidently.
> —Irish, Buck Mulligan said. Is there Gaelic in you?
> —I thought it was Irish, she said, by the sound of it. Are you from the west, sir?
> —I am an Englishman, Haines answered.
> —He's English, Buck Mulligan said, and he thinks we ought to speak Irish in Ireland.
> —Sure we ought to, the old woman said, and I'm ashamed I don't speak the language myself. I'm told it's a grand language by them that knows it.[13]

"Grand" perhaps, but a mere curiosity to all save the English who exploit it for their own amusement. Kinsella's initial version of that same cultural imperialism is devoid of all comedy:

> And the authorities
> Used the National Schools to try to conquer
> The Irish national spirit, at the same time
> Exterminating what they called our "jargon"
> —The Irish Language

Poems, 110

His subsequent attempts at surmounting an Irishman's *trouble aimant de la langue* vacillate between attack and enticement. The attack comes in what might be referred to as Kinsella's public poems, the first of which opened his *Peppercanister* series. "Butcher's Dozen: A Lesson for the Octave of Widgery" is a vituperative poem that denounces in rhymed iambic tetrameter couplets, not the "brutal and stupid massacre" that was Bloody Sunday (the fatal shooting of thirteen demonstrators at Derry on 30 January 1972), but as Kinsella states in an explanatory note to the poem, the decision reached by the investigative committee chaired by Lord Widgery, the Lord Chief Justice. Kinsella denounces the decision as a "cold putting aside of truth, the *nth* in a historic series of expedient falsehoods— with Injustice literally wigged out as Justice."[14]. In 1979, Kinsella reflected on its invective.

> I couldn't write the same poem now. The pressures were special, the insult strongly felt, and the timing vital if the response was to matter, in all its kinetic impurity. Reaching for the nearest aid, I found the *aisling* form—that never quite extinct Irish political verse-form—in a late, parodied guise: in the coarse energies and nightmare Tribunal of Merriman's *Midnight Court*. One changed one's standards, chose the doggerel route, and charged . . .[15]

Here then is what Kinsella calls an essential element of "the Irish tradition . . . an intimate fusion of literature and history." Sensing perfectly when invective serves his purpose, Kinsella has occasionally redeployed the doggerel of the early *Peppercanister Poems,* most effectively in his recent and still ongoing poem, *Open Court.* But as he himself admits, the form has its limits, public poetry as well. He has gone on thus to elaborate a more subtle and far richer strategy of difference.

Kinsella's best and most original work reveals his desire not to wreak verbal vengeance but to obviate cultural hegemony by drawing his reader ever more deeply into his own and Ireland's mythic past. The process involves a deliberate self-estrangement from the very identity the poetry has been striving to create so that the central consciousness of the late work moves, as one of his most perceptive critics has put it, "back and forth between its present state of crisis and confusion and the past sources of its imaginative strength."[16] We are witnessing an attempt, to borrow Philippe Lejeune's metaphor, to give us a behind-the-scenes glance into the workings of the first-person consciousness.

The most audacious instance of this practice comes in a poem where a young couple, caressed by the romance of a summer's day in the country, is making love on a hillside. The poem's consciousness intrudes upon that scene by announcing: "I think this is where I come in." If the strategy of difference has been to impose an ironic presence, the "I" of the poem, who dares here to imagine the very moment of his conception, has succeeded. The shock effect, born out of that most personal of personal moments, is every bit as startling as the frontal attack of Kinsella's public poems. Both strategies work, but this second one, in which Kinsella exploits nostalgia, caressing the language while writing out his fundamental "otherness" within it, is more provocative.

Difference and Identity

Kinsella's profound ambivalence toward the contradictions of his identity can best be appreciated by situating it in terms of the French-language Caribbean writers, Patrick Chamoiseau and Simone Schwarz-Bart. Like Kinsella in his public poems, Chamoiseau condemns the cultural hegemony of post-colonialism by exploiting and attacking the mother tongue that has been foisted upon him. Chamoiseau's bitterly comic satire of administrative pomposity, *Solibo Magnifique,* begins with the discovery of the body of Solibo, the village oracle, whose death seems to be due to a mysterious *égorgette de la parole.* [He had cut his own throat by talking too much.] The official investigation of Solibo's death, complete with pseudo-gymnastic sobriety tests and faked suicide attempts, hinges on a conflict of language and *mœurs* in what might well be a conscious rewriting of Joyce's milkwoman scene from *Ulysses.* Police Superintendant Pilon

and Sergeant Bouaffesse interrogate one of the suspects, who
purports to understand nothing but Creole.

>—Name, first name, nickname, age; occupation, domicile?
>—Huh?
>—Tell us what name people use for you, explained Bouaffesse.
>—Dumbell.
>—That's your nickname? Fine. Now your name and your first
>name.
>—Huh?
>—What did your mother tell City Hall she called you, translated
>Bouafesse.
>—An pa save . . .
>—He says he doesn't know, inspesteur [*sic*] . . .
>—Thank you, Sergeant, but I understand Creole.
>—I said that to help you. You are a police inspesteur [*sic*]; you
>shouldn't be messing around with the patois these vagrants speak.
>—It's a proper dialect, Sergeant.
>—Where'd ya see that?
>—. . .
>—And if it's dialect, how come you're always sounding off in such
>polished French? And why don't you write up your police report
>in it?[17]

Here, as in the passage from *Ulysses*, the master language
delegitimizes the other but cannot eradicate it from memory.
That fact that Bouaffesse deliberately violates both linguistic and
social codes by employing the familiar second person for his
administrative superior and then mangles the pronunciation of
his "hard-won" title only intensifies the uneasy cohabitation of
two cultures and two languages.

Simone Schwarz-Bart takes this uneasy cohabitation as a
starting point but responds to it in profoundly gendered terms,
a strategy that empowers her deceptively serene representation
of alterity in *Pluie et vent sur Télumée Miracle*. In that novel,
the orphan Télumée acknowledges her negritude by recurring
to the fertile enclosure of her own body and to the pregnant
swells and streams that envelop her every movement on the
island. The sensous rhythm of Télumée's speech serves to intensify the suffering that that speech represents, as in the scene
where Télumée first recognizes the ubiquity and the inevitabil-
ity of postcolonial cultural hegemony.

We were protected, learning to read, to write our names, to respect
the flag of France, our mother, to venerate her greatness, her maj-

esty, her nobility, her glory which dates back to the beginning of
time, when we were no more than short-tailed monkeys.[18]

Télumée continues to muffle her private hurt, just as she does
the burden of her meager belongings in that fertile and protective center of her difference—"My clothing wrapped up in piece
of sack-cloth, my sorrow folded up deep down inside me, I took
to the road . . ."[19] Her struggle against the negation of self-
estrangement is so absolute that the structure of the novel could
not be other than circular. Having begun her story at its enigmatic ending—"If I were given the choice it's here, in Guade-
loupe, that I'd choose to be reborn, to suffer and to die"[20]—
Télumée ends it where she had begun—"but I'll die here, the
way I am, standing, in my little garden, what joy!"[21]

Circular Progress

Nothing could be further from Patrick Chamoiseau's vitriolic
fun-making, but it is Schwarz-Bart's gendered approach to difference that helps to illuminate Kinsella's latest work. Just as
Télumée writes out her destiny in terms of her body, so Kinsella's
poet makes woman his muse and repeatedly takes refuge, often
tinged with revulsion, in her "otherness": in the estrangement
of the acrid and suffocating blackness of a grandmother's
aprons, in the whispering of gossiping aunts, and in the enigmatic topos, woman/chicken/egg. Just as Télumée's universe, in
an echo of Julia Kristeva's concept of "Women's Time," blends
past, present, and future into a seamless, timeless whole, so
Kinsella has chosen to become deliberately "Circular-Tending,/
Self-Reflecting."
Such a process might suggest self-indulgence, but Kinsella
obviates any such excess with his hilariously irreverent portrait
of the poet as hero.

> Nine are the enabling elements
> in the higher crafts
> and the greatest of these is Luck.
>
> I lift my
> baton and my
> trousers fall.[22]

Unable to orchestrate his difference into something heroic, the poet refuses to abdicate and goes on instead to imagine a Yeatsian sort of "foul rag and bone shape of the heart," a

> solitary response, eliciting
> order from the uproar of particulars
> struggling toward a posture of refusal
> on the basis of some kind of understanding,
> Man's beggar rags in tatters in the tempest.[23]

That the order of this understanding will be circular, that Kinsella's latest strategy is to return obsessively to the same material, finds its justification in the figure of Aogán Ó Rathaille, one of the major figures of poetry written in the Irish language. Presiding emblematically over Kinsella's meditation on the "Hero as liberator," Ó Rathaille embodies the muteness and the essential isolation of *The Dispossessed*, Kinsella's evocative title for his volume of translations from the Irish:

> Aogán Ó Rathaille defined his part
> at the Western ocean's edge. A vagrant, turning
> the gale wailing inland off the water
> into a voice responding in his head,
> and answering the waves on their own terms
> —energy of chaos and a shaping
>
> counter energy in throes of balance.[24]

Nothing could be more charged than the figure of a poet affronting the very limits of civilization, yet nothing could be more mute than a poet whose words are condemned to battle the howling elements because no one understands his language. Here, though, by evoking the fecundity rather than the futility of this endless and eminently gendered give and take, Kinsella empowers Ó Rathaille's "wailing" and finds in it the very emblem of his difference.

Notes

1. Thomas Kinsella, *Poems 1956–1973* (Wake Forest, Ill.: Wake Forest University Press, 1979), 103. Hereafter abridged to *Poems*.
2. David Lloyd, *Anomalous States* (Durham, N.C.: Duke University Press, 1993), 4.
3. Dominique Deblaine, "La Loquèle antillaise," *Littérature* 85 (février 1992), 81.

4. Thomas Kinsella, W. B. Keats, "The Irish Writer," in *Yeats, Davis, Mangan, Ferguson?: Tradition and the Irish Writer* (Dublin: Dolmen, 1970), 63.

5. Taffy Martin, interview with Thomas Kinsella, Laragh, 18 December 1992.

6. Maxine Hong Kingston, "A Song for a Barbarian Reed Pipe," in *The Woman Warrior* (New York: Vintage Books, 1977), 191.

7. Elyette Benjamin-Labarthe, *Vous avez dit Chicano* (Bordeaux: *Editions de la Maison des Sciences de l'Homme d'Aquitaine*, 1993), 16.

8. Edward Said, *The World, the Text and the Critic* (Cambridge, Mass.: Harvard University Press, 1983), 9.

9. Thomas Kinsella, *Notes from the Land of the Dead and Other Poems* (New York: Knopf, 1973), 55.

10. Thomas Kinsella, *The Táin* (Oxford: Oxford University Press, 1990), xiv.

11. W. B. Yeats, *The Autobiography* (New York: Collier Books, 1967), 45.

12. Daniel O'Hara, *Tragic Knowledge: Yeats's Autobiography and Hermeneutics* (New York: Columbia University Press, 1981), 72.

13. James Joyce, *Ulysses* (New York: Random House, Vintage Books, 1981), 14.

14. Thomas Kinsella, *Peppercanister Poems, 1972–1978* (Wake Forest, Ill.: Wake Forest University Press, 1979), 142.

15. Thomas Kinsella, "Commentary," *Butcher's Dozen*. Reissued 19 April 1992 as Peppercanister 1 (Dublin: Dedalus Press, 1992), 21.

16. Daniel O'Hara, "Review Essay," *Eire-Ireland* 14, 1 (Spring 1979), 132.

17. Patrick Chamoiseau, *Solibo Magnifique* (Paris: Gallimard, 1988), 142–143. My translation.

18. Simone Schwartz-Bart, *Pluie et vent sur Télumée Miracle* (Paris: Seuil, 1972), 81. My translation.

19. Ibid., 89.

20. Ibid., 11.

21. Ibid., 249.

22. Thomas Kinsella, *Her Vertical Smile* (Dublin: Peppercanister, 1985), 25.

23. Thomas Kinsella, *Personal Places* (Dublin: Peppercanister, 1990), 27.

24. Ibid., 27.

Works Cited

Benjamin-Labarthe, Elyette. *Vous avez dit Chicano*. Bordeaux: Éditions de la Maison des Sciences de l'Homme d'Aquitaine, 1993.

Chamoiseau, Patrick. *Solibo Magnifique*. Paris: Gallimard, 1988.

Deblaine, Dominique. "La Loquèle Antillaise," *Littérature* 85, (février 1992), 81–102.

Joyce, James. *Ulysses*. New York: The Modern Library, 1961.

Kingston, Maxine Hong. "A Song for a Barbarian Reed Pipe," *The Woman Warrior*. New York: Vintage Books, 1977.

Kinsella, Thomas. *Her Vertical Smile*. Dublin: Peppercanister, 1985.

———. Interview by Taffy Martin with the poet. Laragh, 18 December 1992.

———. *Notes from the Land of the Dead & Other Poems*. New York: Knopf, 1973.

———. *Peppercanister Poems 1972–1978*. Wake Forest, Ill.: Wake Forest University Press, 1979.

———. *Personal Places*. Dublin: Peppercanister, 1990.

———. *Poems 1956–1973*. Wake Forest, Ill.: Wake Forest University Press, 1979.

——— and W. B. Yeats. "The Irish Writer," *Yeats, Davis, Mangan, Ferguson?: Tradition and the Irish Writer*. Dublin: Dolmen, 1970.

———. *The Táin*. Oxford: Oxford University Press, 1990.

Kristeva, Julia. "Le temps des femmes," *Critical Theory Since 1965*. Ed. Hazard Adams and Leroy Searle. Gainsville, Fla.: Florida State University Press, 1986.

Lloyd, David. *Anomalous States*. Durham: Duke University Press, 1993.

O'Hara, Daniel T. "Review Essay," *Eire-Ireland* 14, 1 (spring 1979), 132.

———. *Tragic Knowledge: Yeats's* Autobiography *and Hermeneutics*. New York: Columbia University Press, 1981.

Said, Edward. *The World, the Text and the Critic*. Cambridge, Mass.: Harvard University Press, 1983.

Schwarz-Bart, Simone. *Pluie et vent sur Télumée Miracle*. Paris: Seuil, 1972.

Yeats, William Butler. *The Autobiography*. New York: Collier Books, 1967.

Index

176